A COMPLETELY DIFFERENT GAME

A COMPLETELY DIFFERENT GAME

My Leadership Playbook

EMMA HAYES

WITH **MICHAEL CALVIN**

PIATKUS

PIATKUS

First published in the US in 2024 by PublicAffairs,
an imprint of Hachette Book Group, Inc.

First published in Great Britain in 2024 by Piatkus

Originally published as *Kill the Unicorn* in audio format by Audible in 2023.

1 3 5 7 9 10 8 6 4 2

A CIP catalogue record for this book
is available from the British Library.

ISBN: 978-0-34944-325-6 (hardback)
ISBN: 978-0-34944-326-3 (trade paperback)

Typeset in Stempel Garamond by Amnet Contentsource
Printed and bound in Great Britain by
Clays Ltd, Elcograf S.p.A.

Papers used by Piatkus are from well-managed forests
and other responsible sources.

MIX
Paper | Supporting
responsible forestry
FSC® C104740

Piatkus
An imprint of
Little, Brown Book Group
Carmelite House
50 Victoria Embankment
London EC4Y 0DZ

An Hachette UK Company
www.hachette.co.uk

www.littlebrown.co.uk

This book is dedicated to my family

Contents

A COMPLETELY DIFFERENT GAME

Prologue

Talking about a Revolution

It was Friday, October 6, 2023, the day after my father's funeral. I could think of nothing else but his passing. I was grieving, in shock, and on autopilot as I got into the car for the crushingly familiar two-hour drive to work at Chelsea FC's training ground.

I knew that once I had negotiated traffic on the A406 and A40, two of London's main arterial roads, I would be blinded by a low winter sun as I merged onto the M25 motorway, the London Orbital. Sure enough, even though I was wearing sunglasses, I had to strain to sit higher, to shield my eyes with the windshield visor.

As I drove, all I could hear was my dad, Sid, in my ear. "You've got to go to that interview, girl," he told me, with such urgency and clarity that he could have been sitting alongside me in the passenger seat. "This is the opportunity of a lifetime."

It is all very well, on sober reflection, to talk about the power of the imagination and the delicate process of mourning a loved one, but to my mind he had basically given me his blessing to put myself forward for the biggest job in women's football, managing the US Women's National Team (USWNT).

I quickly called Jo Tongue, my agent, and said, "My dad has just spoken to me. Put me on the early evening flight to New York on Monday. Tuesday is my day off, so I'll return overnight and be back for work on Wednesday."

I'd asked to be kept in the loop following an informal conversation with the US Soccer Federation after that summer's World Cup in Australia. I had a phone call on my mum's birthday, September 5, from Matt Crocker, their sporting director, who wanted the opportunity to sit down and talk to me.

He made it clear there was a process the Federation intended to follow. They were to use a recruitment agency to gauge the emotional intelligence of candidates before an in-person interview in New York. I told them my head was in the wrong place at that moment. My dad was dying, and I couldn't be anywhere else but by his side.

Matt and his senior colleagues were persistent in keeping the conversation going. My dad passed on September 18. Obviously, I thought of nothing else beyond that . . . until his posthumous, spiritual intervention. We tied at Manchester City thanks to Guro Reiten's ninety-sixth-minute equalizer on the Sunday after my dad's funeral. Once the debrief and warm down was complete, the following day, I flew to New York.

New York is a city I am familiar with. I love it. I lived there for almost seven years. There is a feeling of home when I go there. I checked into the hotel around 10:00 p.m., looked out on to Fifth Avenue, and thought of how many times I had walked up and down it when I was a young coach eking out a $30,000 a year contract.

New York can be a really lonely place. Everything is so tight in the apartments. Kitchens are very small, unlike in London where they are a social space. Kitchens in New York apartments are not places you congregate in, so people tend to go out to eat, even on their own.

I would kill time on my day off by walking endlessly, dropping into coffee shops and exploring the galleries. You have your best times when you have no money and no responsibility. That night, I realized my life was in such a different place now. I had Harry, my beautiful boy, and I was in a suite in a posh hotel, preparing to be interviewed for the most important job in the world.

I felt terribly guilty about being there because of the loyalty I felt I owed my club, my team, and my family, who were going through a hard time. The Federation had left me a lovely welcoming message and a gift box crammed with treats. They evidently felt my pain.

These were people-first people. They had passed a fundamental test of leadership. They cared.

I had to go through a series of assessments the next morning, starting with a timeline of what I considered the five most important events in my life, the first being the trauma of the injury that curtailed my playing career.

It all unfolded quite naturally from there: Going to the US as a young coach. Enduring setbacks in Chicago. Building Chelsea. Having Harry. The importance of my family, a distinctive thread, was woven throughout my recollections.

We spoke about how I had applied the lessons of my life to coaching before I was given fifteen minutes to prepare for a videoconference with the sporting director of a fictitious club, Chicago United, who was refusing to send two of his players to a nonmandatory training camp outside the FIFA timeframes.

I had ten minutes to persuade him to change his mind but instinctively knew that I was never going to get anything done with someone I didn't know in such a short span of time. Instead, I used my time to persuade him to agree to a longer follow-up call. I spoke from a position of empathy and listened to his perspective. I thought it was the most realistic thing to do.

I then talked the interview panel through my playing principles and philosophies, before they set me a task around a game, giving me clips, and asking how they would inform my management of half time.

It was all hypothetical and, inevitably, a little artificial. I chose to concentrate on processes rather than specifics. There is certain language in tone and substance that I would not use in such naturally pressurized situations.

The following sequence, an exploration of my personal journey, had me in intermittent fits of tears since the death of my dad was still so raw. I was really honest with them about my love for Chelsea, and I told them that it was hard for me to even be in the room at that moment. I'm not the sort who interviews for other jobs, but I really appreciated how they had courted me. They respected the position I was in. They did not push me at any point. They made me feel valued.

I flew home and got a call within a day or so offering me the job. I was in my extended kitchen with Lisa Cole, a close friend from my early days in the US, at the time. It was such an exciting moment and strangely appropriate that Lisa should be there, on my sofa, to share it.

We were catching up after the World Cup in Australia. She was the technical adviser to the Zambian team, which had won one of its three matches in its first finals. A former Fiji national coach who has worked in Papua New Guinea, she is best known as the long-term assistant to the late Tony DiCicco, whose transformational US teams were Olympic champions in 1996 and World Cup winners in 1999.

I initially operated with Lisa, who also served as head coach of the Boston Breakers of the National Women's Soccer League (NWSL), at a regional level in the US, identifying talent of potential value to the national team. Progression would come through a club, state, and region in an Olympic development program that selected the best young players from New York to as far south as Delaware and as far north as Maine.

I am not one of those coaches who progressed seamlessly from a pro team in England to a pro team in the States. I went from the amateur game in England and worked up through every level until I became a pro coach. I have always felt accepted in the US because I feel the people I have worked with or coached against understand I have put the hard yards in. They identify with the journey. They appreciate that I know the system from bottom to top, albeit having been out of it for a few years by this point in time.

Lisa was as excited as me by the opportunity that had presented itself. She was energized by the prospect of change at the right time, for the right reasons. "You're the only one who is going to change it," she exclaimed. "You are the only one who is going to revolutionize the system so that it is football first."

I was anxious about the scale of the challenge, to be honest. She reassured me that I was the perfect fit because of my natural ability to work on development strategies and my relationships with clubs in the NWSL and the United Soccer League (USL), the new pro league. Leaders must see a bigger picture than most.

Things were moving fast. Matt asked to meet with me in London the following Sunday, together with Cindy Parlow

Cone, the US Soccer Federation president, and JT Batson, the CEO. I agreed, since Chelsea was to play on the Saturday before (a 2–0 win over West Ham, as it turned out).

The delegation shared their vision and the work they had been doing in the background. It was really impressive. They made me feel really wanted. Their offer—to make me the world's highest paid manager in the women's game—was unbelievable.

Money has never been the most important thing for me, but it was nice to be valued. By adhering to the principle of equal pay—I was to be on the same level as Gregg Berhalter, the men's manager—they also proved they were willing to act on fundamental beliefs.

Despite the disappointment of the earliest US exit from a World Cup, in round sixteen, a new generation of richly talented young players would be coming through. This would be my opportunity to build and lead a team through an Olympic Games, a World Cup, and another Olympic cycle. I couldn't get the thought of this opportunity out of my head, but there were considerations.

I told them I didn't want to leave Chelsea immediately because I had committed to the players. That's the sort of person I am. My word is a condition, an article of faith. I wanted to complete the season in England before attacking the challenge of the Paris Olympics.

I explained that for the first time in my life I was not going to do something at all costs. I did not want to disrupt Harry midway through a school year. I wasn't leaving my mum: she needed me. I would have 100 percent walked away if they had said no.

I couldn't believe how accommodating they were. They acknowledged the logic of my stance, even though they knew they would take some heat domestically because of it. By the same token, if Chelsea had preferred to move on quickly, in terms of succession planning, I would have gone to the US without hesitation.

Leaders do not have the luxury of idle gestures. By finishing the European season, I knew how hard I would have to work to be completely present. I never want to be accused of having stopped working or having switched off. I really believe in professional commitment.

Keeping Twila Kilgore (or Kaufman, as many of us still know her) as the interim head coach was a really smart decision. The first US-born woman to earn a US Soccer Federation pro coaching license, she had spent the previous eighteen months as Vlatko Andonovski's assistant.

She represented continuity and authority because she embodied the strengths of the system, having excelled at the youth, collegiate, and club level. She was able to implement many short-term decisions so that I could hit the ground running when I started in June.

I made it clear how much I valued her, insisting that every department would go through her while I was still a full-time employee of Chelsea. There is always a temptation to gravitate toward a new head coach, but I wanted to be in the background, getting staffing and protocols in place.

A leader's best work is not necessarily splashed over flattering headlines or pored over by an audience of millions. I did a lot of quiet strategic work with the US team in snatched spare time around my duties at Chelsea. It was my role in the interim to set the tone for camps and organize the roster while devolving day-to-day responsibility.

I had initial one-on-one phone conversations with those I left out of the first squad in November. I owed them the professional courtesy of personally explaining the rationale behind their exclusion while stressing that until the early summer their subsequent interactions would be with Twila.

You only get one opportunity to make an initial impression. I knew I had to hit them between the eyes during that first camp. In addition to gathering the entire staff and the twenty-six–strong playing squad, I invited all of the excluded players to attend my presentation via videoconference.

Not a single person was absent.

I used the transcript of an interview with the press officer that would never be released—it was designed as a contingency should Chelsea have chosen not to let me finish the season—as the basis of the hype video. It lasted for barely more than two minutes but had taken two weeks to compile.

It started with me talking over a portentous, prolonged note on an organ: "This is a huge honor to be given the opportunity to coach the most incredible team in world football. I have dreamed about doing this job. You can't turn the US National Women's Team down.

"There is no denying the gaps have closed in the world game, so it is important we work hard to make sure we are on top of the podium. Playing on a team is really simple. Everyone wants to win. To win the biggest things, we have to make the most of those special moments. There will be intense periods, of that I have no doubt. But we will go into competitions with everyone feeling in their best possible place to perform."

The background music became upbeat.

"We've got work to do. It's a healthy form of competition. Nobody has a right to play on the team. It has to be earned from day one. I want to see those good habits, on and off the pitch. I look forward to setting you that challenge. I look forward to building relationships with you, finding out what is important to you, what matters to you, what motivates and inspires you."

Then suddenly, a slower tempo. Pictures of recent matches were undercut by the soulful, seductive lyrics of Tracy Chapman's signature song, "Talkin' 'bout a Revolution." This would be a completely different game, played by a distinctive team.

I told the players my job was to teach them "to understand that if you want to be the best, if you want to be the absolute best, your devotion and dedication to that ambition has to be better and bigger than anything you've ever done before."

I scanned the room, made as much eye contact as possible, and continued: "The success of the very best, whoever they are, whatever they do, is not luck. It is not something that is just handed to you. It is something you have to work so incredibly hard for."

I threw up a pivotal caption: "New Identity. New History. New Heights."

Images of collective success, highlighted by moments of individual exhilaration, spoke for themselves, but I wanted to maintain the urgency of the mood: "It is a huge honor to represent your country. It is my job to bring the best out of you."

We were engaged in something bigger than ourselves. I confronted them with the wise words of Oglala Lakota Chief Henry Standing Bear: "The first warrior looked out at the land that was his home. He saw the hills and the stars, and he was happy.

"For giving him his home, the first warrior told the Great Spirit that he would fight and win many battles in his honor. But the Great Spirit said, 'No, do not fight for me. Fight for your tribe, fight for the family born to you, fight for the sisters you find. Fight for them, for they are your home.'"

The reaction—complete silence—was powerful. I could feel the energy in the room. It was palpable. I then stressed the level of preparation I intended to oversee, the tweaking of our vision and objectives that would continue when they returned to their clubs.

I made it personal, posting visuals of the London streets on which I had grown up. I showed them my Chelsea family, players, and staff who had been a massive part of my life. I spoke about how tough it was to leave them, and I lost myself in the wonder of my little man, Harry.

I told them about my dad ringing me from the Rose Bowl in California at the 1999 World Cup final where, typically, he was trading tickets. I was at Liverpool Hope University at the time; that tournament was my introduction to an iconic US team. I can still hear his enthusiasm: "Emma, you've got to come to America. It's unbelievable, girl. More than ninety thousand at their games. I've not known anything like it."

It wasn't lost on anyone in the room that the gold medal victory over China, 5–4 in a shoot-out, produced perhaps the most legendary image in women's sport: Brandi Chastain celebrating her winning penalty by pulling off her jersey to reveal her sports bra.

People don't remember time. They remember moments.

How would we make our mark? I wanted my players to have five specific qualities. They needed to be count-on-able, coachable, competitive, consistent, and caring. I would focus on creating an environment around that by building up individual profiles.

Everything, I promised, would be intentional. I am not the sort of coach who does football drills because they are fun. That's nonsensical. Everything we do has to be real. For example, take a goalkeeper in a penalty shoot-out. When she gets there, she can't operate on instinct; everything has to be so well-rehearsed.

Another caption underlined this message: "Our culture is to revolutionize and redefine what we are." That complemented another key statement of intent: "We are all on the team but only eleven start. We must all ask, 'What is in the best interests of the team?'"

At that camp we started to identify key words to convey our culture and intentions. The word *electric* kept coming up. The players wanted their style to be dynamic and electric. I just loved that. The fact that it was prompted by one of my young players, NWSL Rookie of the Year Jenna Nighswonger, was an added bonus.

Everyone always says they can feel my passion. It's visceral, without question. What you will always get from me is absolute clarity. As much as there is so much of me that can be maverick, creative, and off the cuff, never forget a fundamental fact of my life.

There's always a plan. Here's mine.

Chapter 1

Kill the Unicorn

When people meet me, I usually get one of three responses. It's either "my mum loves you," which makes me chuckle; "you're an inspiration," which makes me blush; or "you're a legend," which fries my brain. A legend? What the hell is a legend? For me, watching with my son Harry, Thor is a legend, fighting with the Guardians of the Galaxy team. I'm just a football coach, another harassed mother, and, I'd like to think, a woman of the world.

Trust me, I'm no superhero.

I can understand why some find me relatable, because I've never tried to be anyone or anything I'm not. At heart, I'm still the girl from the Curnock Street Estate in Camden. I'm not afraid of grafting. I try to be candid and honest. My instinct is to be inclusive; I'm uncomfortable with being lauded for simply doing my job.

What I'm not is a unicorn. The concept of a head coach or leader as this magical creature, able to solve any problem for their team or company, is unrealistic and ultimately unproductive. If I have a strength, it is in recognizing and repurposing weakness. We've got to kill the unicorn, challenge the perception of a leader's perfection. It's a modern media myth, designed to create a narrative around successful teams and organizations. If you believe the secret of leadership is as simple as relying on one god or goddess, give my love to the fairies at the end of your garden. Organizations outlive leaders, as long as the right framework is in place.

I trust this won't get me banned from X (formerly Twitter), but let's take Elon Musk as an example. He's hailed as a visionary, a guru, a genius. He's reportedly also the first person ever to lose an estimated $180–200 billion of his net worth following a slump in the value of Tesla shares. Even his fan base would concede that's suboptimal. All leaders make poor decisions at some point in their careers because they are human, and none of us have a crystal ball.

Perhaps it's best not to believe the hype. To me, there is nothing more dangerous than the unilateral thinking that comes with slavish devotion to one leader. At its most extreme, it produces monsters such as Adolf Hitler and Vladimir Putin.

In everyday life unilateral thinking stifles creativity, deters debate, and encourages intellectual cowardice. The reality is that the most effective modern institutions—and the best sports teams—have a multidisciplinary, multifunctional approach. Outstanding performance in any field is rarely achieved in isolation. Operating in silos, in which staff work independently without sharing best practice and pivotal information undermines from within.

An integrated approach ensures that I, as a coach and leader, have the capability to assess my players on a number of levels. I need to be aware of the physiological, biomechanical, psychological, medical, and nutritional issues that can limit their impact. Everyone sees things differently through the prism of their specialism, but their expertise is complementary. The physiologist concentrates on matters of flesh and blood. The biomechanist studies angles, speed, and technique. The psychologist gauges confidence, attitude, and personality. These three specialists and other support staff members blend their skills and share the same goals.

I'm not saying the perception of the leader, at the epicenter of everything, is unjustified. I wouldn't deny the importance of a CEO-type figure, who can be critical to how the commercial, competitive, or corporate machine operates.

But if the foundations around that powerful individual are not built properly, cracks will appear. The organization needs underpinning, like a house suffering from subsidence. Interdependence is the mortar that bonds a structure together.

Take my own situation as a starting point. When I met with my team at Chelsea FC after taking time off to deal with some health issues (which I'll touch on a little later), they said they might not have coped well with my absence previously. But they didn't just survive without me. They thrived. The principles we had embedded over time and the values we subscribed to provided a sustainable framework. They progressed because my coaches and support staff grew into the gap I had left.

Do I screw up? On a daily basis, in so many different ways. To be a top performer—to be a leading manager in any sport, business, or endeavor—you have to be prepared to consistently acknowledge your shortcomings. Winning is one way to guarantee longevity—I'm just a contributor to that process—but it is not the only factor.

Although men's sports in particular are still plagued by Neanderthal attitudes, I believe that in football we are at a tipping point of generational change. More leaders are showing their humanity because they must meet modern managerial expectations. It's a simple case of emotional evolution. If you are not a people person, an empathetic manager, you will eventually be spat out of the system. A younger workforce is naturally curious, instinctively questioning, and sees through the unicorn fantasy that one exalted individual has the sole power to change their fortunes. Lasting success is built on teamwork.

The trend toward emotionally intelligent managers goes beyond obvious examples such as Jürgen Klopp at Liverpool. Emotional intelligence—in essence, the ability to manage both your own emotions and understand the emotions of people around you—is just one of the superpowers a great manager needs. The principle of human interaction forms part of the DNA of agile, responsive Premier League clubs such as Brentford and Brighton, as it does in any successful organization.

Brentford has a distinctive culture that dictates the hiring of coaches that fit stylistically and mathematically into the club's business model. Yet, without a shadow of a doubt, that culture is underpinned by a great people manager, Thomas Frank. I'm always very impressed by Thomas whenever I hear him speak. He's loose but incisive, sensitive but forceful. He knows what he wants, and is true to what he believes in.

It's easy to imagine his players buying into his personality as readily as they respond to his philosophy. Similarly, I have no doubt that Roberto De Zerbi was hired by Brighton & Hove Albion FC because he had the profile of someone who could fit seamlessly into the model that brought the best out of Graham Potter, a notably engaged leader. The fact that he was the only candidate they interviewed when Graham left for a brief spell at Chelsea tells you everything you need to know.

British football has modernized its approach to coaching over the past decade, putting it ahead of Spain, France, and Italy. British football may still trail Germany, where holistic attitudes are central to their coach development program, but the level of analytical and scientific innovation is unmatched.

It is fashionable to wonder whether an autocratic figure such as Sir Alex Ferguson could manage effectively in today's game, in which many elite players are indulged by self-serving entourages, fostering the belief they are global, market-sensitive brands.

All things considered, though, I believe Sir Alex would adapt to any challenge, in any era. Although his "hairdryer treatment" of individuals and teams who fell below expected standards has entered football folklore, the timeless nature of his management style is captured by the simplicity of his wisdom. I sat next to him at a League Managers Association awards dinner, when Richard Bevan, the LMA's chief executive, was making his introductory speech. "What do you see?" he asked me, quietly.

My mind raced. It had to be some sort of test, didn't it? I blustered about the measured nature of Richard's leadership, and the value of the support he offered those of us on the front lines. Sir Alex nodded sagely and repeated the question.

"What do you see?" I had to admit I had little more to add. "Look at his hands," he said, directing my attention to the rubber band that Richard was flexing between his fingers. I had assumed it was an aid to concentration, but that missed Alex's broader point about the importance of developing powers of observation.

Managers, leaders in all fields of business must have 20/20 vision, an unerring eye for the type of detail that reveals more than the individual intends. I realize this may sound presumptuous, but the best leaders have an insight into the human condition. It was ironic that my lesson was administered during an awards dinner.

An appreciation of the importance of teamwork is vital. There's nothing more cringeworthy than standing up to take applause and receive a shiny trophy when you are acutely aware others deserve to be there with you. It's so awkward for me because I know that Denise Reddy, the most senior of my assistant coaches, has spent countless unseen hours making people work better.

We won things at Chelsea because of the full range of my players' talents, from Millie Bright's clearheaded defending to Sam Kerr's ability to put the ball in the net. There are so many more people on and off the pitch that I could mention. I'd be nowhere without them. The direction of a team might be shaped by my strengths, but there are so many things the team needs that I can't give them.

My shortcomings are not considered when they hand out Manager of the Month or even Manager of the Season awards. Would we have won sixteen trophies in the last nine years at Chelsea if it was all down to me? No chance.

There's no question that most of us are uncomfortable with being singled out in that manner. That's why we try to reflect the glory toward the assistants and support staff who do the unheralded grunt work.

There's so much ambiguity in football management. For starters, what do you call me? In England, I was called the manager—although *manager* and *coach* may be used interchangeably. In the US, I was called the head coach. I view my role as closer to that of a CEO or a head contractor, even though I get my boots dirty on the grass, like all coaches. People tell me all the time that my job is about winning matches. I understand that, but the facilitation of my team, and the team around that team, is absolutely critical.

What do I do if I have a player with a persistent illness that requires major medical intervention? How can I help the finisher who hasn't scored in five games and needs individual work on the training ground? When do I connect a player whose confidence is at rock bottom with the analyst who has evidence of her ability, a clip showing all of the goal assists she has contributed over the last two years?

The importance of the coordination of the team may as well be written in invisible ink as far as most external observers are concerned. Yet, as a manager you have to face the reality that someone has to be held accountable. When the team wins, the players get the credit. When it loses, it is the manager's fault.

Managers get used to being hung out to dry. Resilience comes with the territory because knockbacks are a daily occurrence. There aren't many professions that involve dealing with such self-focused individuals as professional athletes. As a leader, you develop a distance while remaining close enough to smell their fears and sense their problems.

You work every day as if it is your last in the job. There's no respite, even when you enjoy a period of success. And it's not even about sustaining that success. You're told it must be taken to another level, regardless of logical possibilities. You know you've disappeared down the rabbit hole when past achievements are held against you.

I understand our role is to help people perform to the best of their ability and on a consistent basis, but we are not miracle workers. We manage human beings. They're capricious creatures, predictably unpredictable.

It's a flesh and blood business. You have to look out for premature deterioration as a player ages. You have to sense the unease of the new player who is struggling to settle in. You have to compartmentalize your own expendability. Whether you currently lead a team or a company, or you're aiming for a promotion, one of the biggest mistakes anyone can make is to believe they have an irreplaceable skill set. You may be unique, but someone else could do your job.

For all the gory tales of boardroom coups in the wider working world, there are few jobs that can match mine in the brutality with which we are kicked to the curb once we have served a certain purpose. It's horrific.

There is no denying that we marginalize people. That's inevitable when you have twenty-odd players, all insistent they deserve to be in the starting eleven. It is inescapable that those starters are going to be given the majority of the coaches' attention.

I tell my players all the time I'm not here to be equal, I'm here to be fair. Equality of opportunity is an illusion. Everyone ticks along when the team is winning, but when performances stutter and results suffer, the knives come out. The subs can agitate for a place in the team with greater force. Every organization has individuals waiting for their chance. Players' agents pursue the profit motive—there's money to be made in instability.

Head coaches are cultural icons in the US, especially in basketball and football. Football (or soccer to US audiences), the world's favorite game, is rather more elemental and inherently tribal. It features often bewildering contrasts. Cults of true believers coalesce around top coaches. They are willfully blind to their faults and turn into attack dogs when their hero's reputation is challenged.

There has been the odd occasion when I've been portrayed as some sort of cross between Mother Teresa and Albert Einstein. That's wide of the mark, by several continents. It reveals a basic misunderstanding of professional sport.

Football is chaos. If anyone thinks it can be orchestrated by these supposed higher beings in their technical areas close to the touchline, they are off their head. I grimace when I hear commentators attempting to rationalize an improved second-half performance, for instance, by speculating about what was said at halftime.

"Ah, I bet Emma had something to say." What a load of rubbish. How do they know? They may be able to detect a marginal influence, but it is so subjective. They have no clue what I said or did. Here's the reality.

The first four minutes of the break is spent with my staff. At Chelsea I would go first to my general manager, Paul Green, who watches from the stand. He delivers a neutral, detached view of how the game is going. We then have input from coaches with responsibility for specific phases—defending, attacking, and set pieces.

The players are simultaneously calming down, having a pee, rehydrating, and talking while the physiotherapists circulate. I go into the dressing room armed with clips from the analyst because visual information is more immediate than verbal communication. I've got four minutes, tops.

It is a mistake to overload the players. I don't refer to passages of play from the first half, other than in generalities. There's no time for aimless effing and jeffing. My biggest job, going into the second half, is usually to get the players out of their own heads.

I may get them up, draw them into a circle, and have them link their arms to get them focused. At least, then, I've got them on the same page. I can influence in the margins, but I cannot control. The idea that as a leader I am in complete command of events doesn't add up. There are times when it feels like I am herding goldfish or trying to chase down a litter of particularly energetic puppies.

No one goes into a match with any degree of certainty. We might think we prepare for every eventuality, but shit happens. A player freezes. You pick the wrong lineup, rely on the wrong play. The opposition do something unexpected. Your responsibility is to recognize what is happening, why it is happening, and when and how you need to respond.

I admire those coaches who won't wait until halftime to make changes, knowing it implies personal fault. It is very difficult to shape events pitchside. Your shouted messages must be short and simple, but the players probably won't hear a word you say. While all this is going on, the cameras are trained on you. An audience of millions is waiting to be impressed or appalled on the flimsiest of evidence.

A CEO of a Fortune 500 company doesn't have a camera pointed at their face in the boardroom when the new business plan is taking shape. A surgeon isn't confronted by a media scrum and expected to supply a pithy quote when walking out of the operating room. A pilot gets away with brief, well-rehearsed and unchallenged platitudes from the cockpit.

I've been around long enough not to be conscious of media intrusion, but our business is so volatile. We veer between alarm, despondency, and unrestrained joy in a matter of minutes. We are subjected to unconscious bias by the media and the fans because judgments are often made on an aesthetic basis. It is easier to praise an imaginative, innovative coach such as Man City's Pep Guardiola than it is to acknowledge the work of a pragmatic coach such as Everton's Sean Dyche, whose teams tend to be less easy on the eye but invariably greater than the sum of their parts.

Guardiola talks about not wanting his players to think he doesn't know what he is doing, even though there must be periods when he hasn't a clue what's going on. We try to cultivate implicit trust, like an officer leading troops into combat. We attempt to soothe any fears in the way passengers instinctively glance at the stewardess for reassurance when a plane goes through turbulence.

You can't fly under the radar. That's why you learn to carefully consider anything you say in public. Yet the more successful you are, the higher profile you have, the bigger temptation there is to project an inaccurate image of yourself. It's important to stay grounded and authentic when the spotlight is on you.

I tell my players to think of me as a bus driver. I've got the headphones on, to phase out a chorus of voices. Forget for a moment the fans and assorted football people. I am also in a profession that is a hobby to friends and family, and they all want their say. Every now and again I'll have a quick listen to opinions and then return to blissful isolation. I'm sustained by the profound honesty you can find within a sports team.

There are parallels with a successful family business: we feel compelled to speak the truth, we annoy one another, but deep down we know we need each other to get by. Somehow, we get on. Every one of my players knows that I'll do absolutely anything I can for them. That doesn't mean that they'll like it, want it, or need it all of the time—far from it. But I try to engage people in the process as much as I possibly can. I'm very proactive.

Football is a profession that should come with a health warning, but so much remains unspoken or unwritten. Which is where this book comes in. I understand the basic contradiction of presenting a blueprint for personal or collective advancement while making a virtue out of weakness and vulnerability, but it comes from the heart.

I'm not expecting you to agree with me or to treat my suggestions as Holy Writ. My aim is to make you think, through the weight of my experience. I know I cannot control perceptions of me, but I try to be transparent and, above all, honest. That seems rare these days.

A less idealistic, more realistic view of leadership is overdue. I hope to provide a clear and practical definition of what that is so you can better direct your own life and career, whatever business you are in. In my eyes, imperfection reflects the human experience. It helps us all to connect. I am far from perfect. I own that daily and admit to errors. I went into sports to rip up convention, and you are welcome to lend a hand by using my ideas in your own field.

Although luck plays a part, it's generally accepted that success is the result of talent, planning, and persistence. But first we've got to challenge the idea that leaders are responsible for our career highs or lows. Whether you own a business, manage a department, or are retraining, the success of your venture will depend on the way your organization is structured—not on a mythic leader.

If the unicorn did exist, scientists believe it was closer to a rhinoceros than a horse. That pretty, pearly white creature with a flowing mane, wings, and a horn depicted in films and found on so many nursery walls is a fantasy.

Choosing the right people and knowing what makes them tick will be integral to your success. Teams, not unicorns, win trophies.

Chapter 2

Remember Your Roots

I don't own a watch, so don't bother asking me the time, but I can't stop the clock. Life acquires occasionally painful clarity as you grow older. I have realized through the cycle of love and loss that I would be nothing without my family.

I grew up in a supportive community on the Curnock Street Estate. We had a corner flat, with a balcony that made up for us never having a garden. Different blocks would play football against each other, twenty to a side with a raggy-arsed ball on the playground.

It was gloriously chaotic. The games stopped when we heard the chimes of the ice cream van. Everyone shouted up to their mums for fifty pence (about seventy US cents)—mine would throw me a coin over the balcony. I can still taste the lemon ice cream with strawberry sauce, my favorite.

We played until it was dark, and I quickly developed a sense of independence. My role, as the middle sister, was to look after our youngest, Rebecca. That meant dealing with conflict and sorting out the estate bully.

I became more aware of professional football players as I entered my teens. I loved Gary Lineker's legs and Gazza's manic laughter. Glenn Hoddle was a magician and ahead of his time, but I was captivated by Diego Maradona—part pirate, part poet, who had beamed down from another planet.

Football was my main means of self-expression. I was the only girl in the primary school team, and a teacher recommended Rebecca and I to a dominant local girls' team, Mary Ward. We won tournaments across London and stored our medals and trophies in cardboard boxes. Winning became second nature.

That's where my mentality to compete and aim high came from. I played with my mates, people I trusted and respected. We worked with and for each other. They understood what made me tick and, to this day, remain my closest friends.

Mary Ward merged with Limehouse Ladies to form the first-ever Arsenal Under-10 team. Vic Akers asked my dad, Sid, to be manager. Arsenal recognized my potential as a creative midfield player and regular goal scorer but becoming a professional football player was an impossible dream. It simply wasn't an option. In those days, everyone was an amateur.

When I was fifteen, life got in the way, in any case. My sliding-doors moment came when I wrecked my ankle in a fall on a mogul run during a school ski trip to the Italian Alps. I had an operation, reinjured it, and was given inserts for my shoes in an attempt to strengthen the area and correct my balance. I got used to living with pain.

I am left-footed and the anklebone had a huge hole in it. The cartilage was being pushed into that hole and it gradually wore away. Every time I planted my foot on the floor, it felt as if the bone was hitting the ground.

Today, there is a good chance it would be repaired through microsurgery, but back then MRIs were limited. The specialist told me I could never kick a ball again. I proved him wrong, to an extent, by playing for Millwall FC and Barnet FC before going to university, but basically went into mourning.

On reflection, I had a wide range of formative experiences that equipped me to do my current job in a certain way. Mum was extremely nurturing, the epicenter of the household. She made sure we ate fresh food every day. I didn't realize Iceland (the supermarket, not the country) existed until I went to university. I'll never forget those frozen crispy pancakes. They looked so nice and tasted so horrible.

I cannot honestly remember doing any school homework, but I clearly had a natural propensity for language. I became interested in current affairs, going to the newsstand each morning to get my mum *The Sun*. Everyone read the sports pages, but I wanted more.

I questioned the world around me from a young age. When I was twelve, Mum would get me the *Guardian* and the *Observer* on Sundays. There was a lot of self-teaching going on. I managed to scrape into higher education because of my thirst for learning and progression.

Today, people tell me I am middle class because of my education and income, but I consider myself to be working class through and through. Social stratification—how we categorize people—is so different these days. My parents built our family in the seventies and eighties when social housing was more commonplace for more of us.

Margaret Thatcher's government passed a housing act that allowed some residents the right to buy their own council houses (public housing built by local authorities). It changed life for some people, but not enough. Whether that is because of low income, low education, or low opportunity, many people remain trapped. Upward mobility is harder than ever.

I was one of the last students to get a grant to go to university, before tuition fees were introduced for higher education students in 1998. I couldn't have gone without it. Mum was upset that she couldn't afford to support me. She appeared in front of the local council, asking for financial help, and told them it was her dream for me to be the first of the family to enter higher education.

Camden High Street was my place to escape our small three-bedroom flat, which, at one stage, contained my two sisters, their boyfriends, and my mum and dad. I lost myself in the music scene, bouncing from the Mango Room to the Oxford Arms, to The Barfly, Underworld, and the Camden Palace, where I sneaked in at the age of fifteen.

I soaked up everything: punk, reggae, ska, soul, indie, and dance. Victoria, my older sister, developed my love for George Michael. She has the gift of the gab and is a great salesperson, like my father. Her flair for the dramatic taught me how to act up on camera if the need arises during a game.

I loved reading and was drawn to the books of the great mescaline-fueled gonzo journalist, Hunter S. Thompson. My youth club in Highgate New Town was not just a place to play pool or table tennis. We had youth workers educating us about the paths we could go down in life.

Mum was a helper. Dad pushed me. His mantra was if I wanted something, I had to earn it. After I completed my schooling and before starting university, I worked for him at Billy Bunters sandwich shop in Jubilee Market Hall in Covent Garden, where he also ran theater ticket and foreign-exchange businesses.

This was before overpriced skinny lattes and sandwich chains such as Pret. I got up at 5:00 a.m. each day to make

500 baguettes and countless sausage rolls. Mum made paninis and chicken and broccoli soup and laid out penny candy. Dad taught me never to take anything for granted.

He ran all the tough youth football teams in Somers Town, between Euston and St. Pancras stations. The kids there, ages sixteen to eighteen, were really challenging, but he kept them out of trouble. He was their role model, and they are now adults with kids of their own.

Dad was also pivotal in setting up the Regents Park League. I helped him develop it with the police when I was working as a sports development coach for the local council during holidays from university. It is still one of my proudest achievements.

The aim of the league was to use football as a way to reduce conflict between the Bangladeshi and Pakistani communities. We formed a dozen teams. The games could get very feisty, and the police presence occasionally came in handy, but the league has flourished: there are now three thousand kids competing every Saturday.

The league is one of my dad's great legacies. When he passed away following a typically defiant battle against cancer, it felt as if my world had fallen apart. It was a pain without equal and without measure.

He left a hole the size of the Grand Canyon. The football community around the world reached out, knowing the magnitude of our loss. Our local newspaper, *Camden New Journal*, devoted its entire front page to his passing. The main headline read, "Sid, Our Champ on the Sidelines"; "Farewell to a Pioneer" ran a strapline.

We returned to Regents Park on a mild Saturday in mid-March 2024, to pay tribute to him. Thousands of kids played in his Memorial Day, on pitches laid out almost as far as the eye could see, I met so many people I grew up with, volunteering, coaching, parenting. It was a joyful community occasion, full of fun and sudden sadness.

I realized how far we had come when I handed out the medals in the girls' tournament. It had taken years to bring the girls' competition into line with that of the boys'. I refereed the adults' memorial match, which featured both sexes and countless individuals who had been dad's disciples. I couldn't play because I was awaiting an injection in my ankle, but reminiscing in a local sports bar afterward, I had a strong sense of being home.

Dad was a special, special man, with a distinctive view of life. Through the tears at his funeral service, I found comfort in what he would have made of it all. He would have been thinking, "Don't waste money on a fancy wooden coffin and a grand farewell. Look after the living."

He looked after us. Boy, did he look after us. He was our world. He taught us to take responsibility, to work hard, and to look after our own. He inspired us to go after whatever we wanted and passed on his instinct for opportunity.

He cared about his community. He loved to fight the establishment. He wasn't slow in calling out the con men. He supported those without power, privilege, and a platform. He was a superhero without a cape.

He gave me the strength to stand up for what I believed in, regardless of the repercussions. He saw things in me that I didn't see in myself. His life was a mosaic of magical memories.

Mum was and is the caring kind. I can see Dad in his favorite leather chair, being spoiled. He only liked home-cooked food. A plate of oysters, some calamari. A nice, thick, juicy steak. No takeout. My earliest football memory is of sitting on the floor in my Tottenham Hotspur tracksuit watching the 1984 UEFA Cup final with him. We'll always have goalkeeper Tony Parks and that tense, triumphant save in the penalty shoot-out, Pups. At eight years old, watching Parks's heroics and the mass celebration they prompted was the most amazing thing I had ever seen.

Life echoes across the generations. My dad and his grandson Harry were as thick as thieves. I saw something of myself in my boy, sitting with his grandfather on the sofa, watching videos on YouTube about steam trains and learning about cars.

Dad's old Mercedes estate car was always full of kids being ferried to matches. I'd find him in the bar after my games, holding mini-coaching sessions. Laughter followed him around because he was a very funny guy.

He was a rebel, and we were his cause. We were banned from playing football in the flat, but he joined in anyway. He took us to watch Barnet, Queens Park Rangers, and Tottenham. But never Arsenal, thank God. The first call I made after every match—as player, coach, or manager—was to him. This was the hardest habit to break.

I'll never forget the day we were arrested in Rotterdam, Netherlands, at the UEFA Euro 2000 finals. As dad and daughter bonding trips go, it was off the scale. I was twenty-three at the time. We were sitting in the main square with other England fans, who were all quite loose after visiting the coffee houses in Amsterdam. A fleet of London cabs turned up, and promotional girls began handing out betting slips.

Before we knew it, one hundred or so riot police came out of nowhere and hauled everyone off to the police station. Dad was apoplectic, telling them to let me go. His temper didn't improve while we were being booked by the station sergeant.

"Why do you want me to remove my fucking belt?" he asked them.

"Because we don't want you to strangle yourself."

Things moved fast when they noticed his Timberland boots. They wanted the laces.

"Why?"

"Because we don't want you to harm yourself."

That was that. Off came his shirt, trousers, underwear, and socks. He stood there stark naked.

"I ain't going to strangle myself," he told them with a mischievous smile. "I want to freeze to death."

I still had my backpack on. I was mortified, but quietly proud. We spent nine hours in adjoining cells before being released without charge.

I need only close my eyes to see that knowing smile. I think of him whenever I smell baby oil. He loved to use it because it somehow put him at ease. That smell reminds me of the softness hidden beneath a hard exterior.

We spent a day laughing, crying, and singing songs from shows when we gathered to remember him as an extended family in a villa in Tenerife at Christmas 2023. He loved the classics: *Les Misérables*, *Cats*, *The Phantom of the Opera*. We set up a little shrine using silver-framed photographs of him and poured out our memories.

Dad wouldn't give me money to go to university because he believed I'd just spend it on beer. A little harsh, and probably fair, but he also urged me to work in the US, the land of opportunity. He knew before I did that it would enable me to build a life.

I took European studies, Spanish, and sociology at Liverpool Hope University, and earned my masters' degree in intelligence and international affairs. It broadened my horizons and developed my powers of reasoning. I understood then how the radicalization of Europe, stimulated by the internet, would blur national boundaries and create a refugee problem.

I am intrigued by European politics post-1945, but my true passion is espionage. I'm fascinated by what it takes to persuade someone to turn against their state and conspire against everything they have ever known or believed in.

I applied to MI5, the UK's security service, to work in national security but did not hear back. Maybe Stella Rimington, MI5's former director, didn't fancy any more female competition.

I spent my gap year interrailing around Europe before deciding to act on another of Dad's formative pieces of advice: I needed to believe in myself regardless of what people say about me or my plans. I was lying in the bath at the time; Rebecca remembers sitting on the toilet, listening to me pour my heart out. I hated the restrictive, self-defensive, brain-dead culture of English football. In the US, I saw a less conventional, more open-minded environment. The women's game was professional in name and nature. Respect had to be earned, but was given regardless of age, sex, or background when the achievement merited it.

I arranged to work in Major League Soccer camps. I bought a $1,000 one-way airline ticket and threw some clothes into a backpack. My sisters drove me to Heathrow Airport, stopping off for a good cry on the way. I was determined not to look back.

I arrived at JFK Airport in New York City, where I was met by someone named Dave. He gave me a set of keys, a map of Long Island, and told me I was scheduled to meet Sue Ryan at 1:00 p.m. the next day at a place called Stony Brook for my first session.

It turned out to be a small coastal settlement. To get there I had to navigate Interstate 495, the Long Island Expressway, on my own. It was simultaneously terrifying and exhilarating, but I'd found my place in the world.

I earned $120 a week for a seven-day week and coached teams around Long Island before taking charge of the Lady Rough Riders in the USL W-League. I was named coach of the year in 2002 after going through the fourteen-game season unbeaten.

It was an unbelievable experience. I learned the importance of relating to a community, the craft of building networks, and began to understand the nuances of my trade. I discovered that ambition was not a dirty word, and that self-confidence was not a sin.

The power of personal contact was paramount in the college system, often sleeping on the couches of friendly coaches during recruitment trips. I had no budget and had to persuade players to commit to me without the benefit of being able to offer them a scholarship. I was basically selling myself.

Leaders learn their most significant lessons from other leaders. Take care to build your own network of trusted allies in your field.

My outlook on coaching was revolutionized by a chance conversation on military tactics at a coaching conference with a stranger who was born in India, had English parents, and had traveled throughout Africa and Europe, where his father worked as an oil executive. I didn't know it at the time, but Anson Dorrance, a former lawyer, had won the inaugural women's World Cup with the US in 1991. As head coach of the

University of North Carolina Tar Heels, he has twenty-two national football titles to his credit. He's one of the most brilliant men I have met.

He blew my mind with his boldness and intuition, handing out a manual that outlined how he worked and why his teams were so successful. My God. I'd never known such audacity. He was telling me how to beat him but he didn't care because he believed in himself and his methods.

I was used to people whispering behind their hands, treating mundanities as state secrets. Anson was basically saying take your best shot. It was massively influential because it taught me never to be afraid of openness. Some of his core values still strike a chord with me. He speaks of nobility, respect, and positivity. He stresses that the truly extraordinary do something every day. His aim is for his staff and players to have lives that contain never-ending ascensions.

One of his central philosophies involves transcending ordinary effort. He argues that too many people work within their own comfort zone. Such ordinary effort, in his eyes, is an admission of mediocrity. I won't lie, he had me hooked. I immediately rededicated myself to working to the best of my ability. That would take priority above everything else.

I have never had a weekend off in my working life. I don't know what that feels like. People laugh when I say there are parallels between being a coach and a nun, whose life is dictated by a single, noble purpose. In my trade, self-sacrifice is inevitable.

It is not up to me to judge whether that is healthy or realistic. That's down to you, by framing your own ambitions and making your own lifestyle choices. All I can do is be as honest as possible in presenting my reality.

I'm naturally entrepreneurial and over the last couple of years I have been working quietly on a boutique foreign-exchange project. This has taken me back more than a decade, when I wanted to help my dad take his business online. He was driven, incredibly creative human being, but I brought to the table a more logical mind.

I developed software systems, built websites, and oversaw back-end content management programs. I loved the combination of technology and process, which taught me one of the key components of successful leadership: without an effective framework to process feedback, opinions can fly all over the place and disrupt your organization.

There is an off switch in most professions. I have the greatest admiration and gratitude for those who teach small children between 8:00 and 3:30 each weekday. They have homework to mark and lessons to plan outside of those hours, but they are not dealing with kids when they do so.

When you are coaching and leading professional athletes there is no respite. You are responsible for their welfare and you are dealing constantly with lifestyle issues of varying degrees. This is taken for granted. Sometimes players get angry with me for making decisions that affect them deeply, but they tend to come back to me at the end of their careers and confess, "I don't know how you put up with it all. I don't know how you did it."

I don't mention this to commend myself. If one of my current or former players found themselves in trouble, I would be there for them in a heartbeat. I'm about helping people in whatever way I can, but football is my muse—it's what drives my passion for the job. A really effective leader isn't just driven by money or status; it's because they love what they do.

Remember,

- leaders learn from other leaders.
- commit to transcending ordinary effort.
- above all, cherish those closest to you.

My dad remains with me, despite being released from his suffering. I read extracts from this book to him because he was proud of it, and I wanted him to know how proud I was of him. I philosophized with him when he was slipping in and out of consciousness. "Why me?" he asked. I'm so sorry I couldn't answer an impossible question.

He chose to leave on his own terms, passing away when my brother-in-law Mark, who spent every day at his bedside in hospital, popped out of the ward for a cup of tea. He left me with a final squeeze of my hand, but I still feel his spirit.

We will keep chatting. I know, wherever he is, he will hear me. I promise I'll continue to listen out for his whispers. Thank you for everything, Pups. And God bless.

Chapter 3

Know Your People

This particular room in the Tate Modern in London is bathed in an eerie indigo-blue light. It hums with the confusing whispers of around eight hundred analog radios of different sizes and ages, each tuned to a different station and arranged in a circular structure.

It took Cildo Meireles, the Brazilian sculptor, ten years to produce what he refers to as "a tower of incomprehension." The noise produced by the artwork is constant and invades the consciousness, but the precise mix of broadcast voices and music is ever-changing. No two experiences of this giant artwork are the same.

Meireles called it *Babel,* after the biblical story of a tower tall enough to reach the heavens. This offended God, who made the Babylonian builders speak in different languages. Their inability to communicate with one another became the source of enduring human conflict that caused them to scatter across the Earth.

What does this have to do with a football team, a sales force, a board of directors, or any group working toward a common goal? Think about it. Radios are like human beings, similar yet unique. Switch them all on at once and the commotion makes communication impossible.

I show my players images of that tower whenever I want to illustrate the importance of our individuality and interdependence. I am trying to tune the frequencies of forty to fifty players and staff members so that they are on the same wavelength.

Professional athletes tend to be very good at putting up a facade, and trying to be who they think you as their leader want them to be. It's tricky to find a way through that little maze, but in my business, there is an eternal, undeniable truth. Name for me another profession in which you could be sacked one week and rehired the next. I'm prepared to wait.

That is the reality facing my players, who are asked to play up to three times a week. Despite all the work on team culture, there is no such thing as a first eleven anymore. I pick from twenty-five players. People are dropped, promoted, and rotated. They have to deal with what I call the try, fail, and adapt process.

There are no certainties. Observers don't always appreciate how lonely, arduous, and confidence-sapping that can be. Modern players have to cope with that while hearing or, more pertinently, listening to what everyone has to say about them.

People are very quick to judge this generation of players for their inability to handle criticism, but do we ever consider how much they are faced with? They're being bombarded with opinions, much of it unsolicited. They get it from the coach, from the parents, from the agents, and from social media. It's coming at players from all angles, all of the time. We had twelve national team captains play for Chelsea in my time at the club. It is a multinational, multicultural environment.

This environment requires an understanding of what different things mean to different people. My interaction with a player is just one element of the human chemistry involved. When the player deals with the team doctor, the sports scientist, the performance coach, or the assistant coach the dynamics will change again. A player can easily be pulled in different, distracting directions, so my major key message is that the best, most successful organizations have the best communications. That gives us clarity of intent and reminds us of our common purpose. It provides the foundation of everything we do.

Discover What Drives Your Team

My team will never be treated as just numbers, even though the players wear them on their back. Leaders must take the time to find out who their people are and what matters to each of them. These individuals are recognizable human beings, contrasting characters with distinctive needs. I will be their most passionate advocate. I will broadcast the impact and importance of their contributions. I'll be there for them when things do not go so well.

Do you know who your colleagues are? What are they driven by? People, processes, or performance?

We start with the assumption that everyone has a common goal: winning. That is an intrinsic motivation that drives us day to day. My team, for the most part, is people-driven. They are people pleasers, the types who do it for the team. I will remind a player with those characteristics of their importance to the group. That feeds into their sense of self-worth and responsibility to others. The best example I can give is Beth England. Introduce her to a game with the reminder that "the team needs you" and she will excel.

I focus on practicalities when a player is more process oriented, someone driven to perfect the structure of the game. I might tell her to concentrate on running behind the opposition defense, or carrying the ball into dangerous areas, or on making the intelligent movement that so often leads to a goal. That connects them to the task at hand. They know if they put one foot in front of the other, they will get to where they want to go, or be.

Performance-driven players are mainly focused on winning the next game, the next season, and the next Cup. There's a wonderful simplicity to that. They are the ones who tell you, "Give me the ball and the team will win." Pernille Harder is a good example of this breed. All I needed to do was tell her "Go out and win us the game."

The specific instruction or encouragement doesn't matter because I know from experience that the player can cope with the processes that produce excellence. Those processes have to evolve constantly, due to the nature of our opposition and natural fluctuations in form. They have to be part of a two-way process.

If I ask you what worked well, I want you to put yourself in my position and tell me what worked well for me too, as your coach. If I ask what didn't work well for you, I want you to tell me what didn't work well for me as well. We initiate discussions like that after every game, so that the result is seen as a consequence of collective actions. Becoming aware of individuals' motivating factors has fundamentally changed the way I coach.

Ensure you understand what drives the people on your team or organization, perfect your systems, and you have every chance of maximizing your team's potential.

We have great, insightful conversations. Players need to know they meet my expectations, and I need to know I meet theirs. I am as transparent and collaborative as possible when it comes to the bonus structure for my team. I ask them how they want the money to be distributed and on what scale within the group. I will incorporate their views into the reviews of my staff. What more do you need from us? How could we do our jobs better? What is the missing link in the coaching, conditioning, or medical departments? What do we need more or less of? How else can we improve our relationships? If you don't tell us, we will never know.

I've been surprised by the variety of things that mattered to people but once I'm aware of them, I can react accordingly. It is not a one-size-fits-all approach.

To give an example, the following exchange involved a member of staff. Due to the ultra-competitive nature of elite sport, there's an automatic assumption that winning is always the most important factor. Money motivates us all, but in this particular case the staff member's primary driver was respect. Our conversation went something like this:

Me: So, how do you want to be heard?
Staff member: I want to be included in the coaching conversations you and Denise have.
Me: What happens if you're not in and Denise and I are having them at nine o'clock at night?
Staff member: Just shoot me a text.

Me: OK. How can I make you feel like you've had a
positive impact?

Staff member: If I've done something well, put a Post-it
note on my computer.

I learned something valuable that day. As a coach I often
assumed that I had expressed respect and made someone feel
valued by saying well done after a game or a particularly productive training session. In this case, in their eyes, it obviously
wasn't as simple as that.

It isn't always going to be sweetness and light. But before
any player or staff member walks into my office, I want to
know what is important to them. Otherwise, I won't be able to
tap into their talent. I need to understand their needs and their
value systems, whatever they may be.

To give another example, I was about to send a young
player, a promising product of the Chelsea development system, out on loan to another club. The most important thing to
her was playing for the Chelsea badge. The second most
important thing was representing the badge in a way that was
honorable for her and her family. That made my messaging
easy.

I was not sending her to another club because I didn't think
she was going to cut it with us in the longer term. I stressed the
importance of her excelling with a new team because it would
reflect well on our club. She would honor the badge by doing
her utmost to develop her talents and make a positive contribution in a different environment.

Such conversations, and the dexterity of management they
require, spill over into my personal life. I get Harry, my son, to
write down what he loves the most and interact accordingly.

That's why I have train sets placed permanently around the house. It's important to him at the moment.

Encourage Conflict Resolution

Actions work two ways. I've got to hold people to account, and I expect to be held to account myself. My priority is to avoid passive-aggressive behavior, which is a killer in every business. I'd argue that conflict is actually conducive to successful working environments, although it cannot be sustained. One of the toughest jobs for a leader is to know when to mediate. Conflict between employees is not unhealthy if it is managed in the right way.

All coaches and leaders are magpies, collectors of shiny things. I show my players videos of team meetings held by Kara Lawson, head coach of the women's basketball team at Duke University. She was a successful professional player and broadcaster and worked in the National Basketball Association as an assistant coach for the Boston Celtics. Her core preseason message involves commitment to one another. She tells her players how to do so and why it matters fundamentally.

To know your teammates, you must commit to spending time with them. You will share and reflect contrasting emotions because the journey you are undertaking is long and challenging. One of the biggest misconceptions of great teams is that they never have problems, despite considering the group as an extended family and cherishing a collective culture.

Any leader who insists their people never fight among themselves is, to be charitable, stretching the truth or trying to keep up appearances. It might be that they just haven't fought yet. Conflict is a pivotal part of a successful team, but the key difference is that anger and pettiness are not allowed to linger. Commit to one another and move past it.

Here's Kara's approach, in a nutshell: "We all wait for things to get easier. Life is going to get easier. Basketball is going to get easier. School is going to get easier. It never gets easier. What happens is you become someone who handles hard stuff better. If you think life when you leave college is going to all of a sudden get easier because you graduated, and you've got a Duke degree, it's not. It's going to get harder, so make yourself a person that handles hard well."

I love the tone of her delivery. It's confident, challenging, and supportive. Above all, it acknowledges an uncomfortable truth. We must not bubble wrap the younger generation. We cannot remove all the obstacles in their way. If we could do so, by some sort of magic, it would do more harm than good, because they then wouldn't have the necessary resilience to deal with unexpected challenges.

Do we teach our people how to coach themselves? At Chelsea, we realized that we didn't. To address this, we concentrated on teaching people how to ask for support. We told them to go to a variety of sources rather than go to the coaching staff for reflection, and instead of asking their friends what they can do better we encouraged them to ask the person they liked the least.

Once they were prepared to make that leap of faith, we worked on reducing their defensiveness. They had to learn to embrace the truth. Hear what you want to hear, by all means, but you have to analyze yourself. You have to be self-critical, otherwise feedback is useless.

How many players on teams are filling a space? They may be getting paid but are they contributing? By that I don't just mean on the pitch, but off it as well. Ask searching questions of your teammate. Team building involves difficult conversations, and challenging circumstances.

I often tell individuals, "If you are not enabling the team, you're sabotaging us." I'll accept you might be an introvert and more comfortable staying in the background, but reticence doesn't necessarily create the mutual trust we require. I'll also accept that, as an extrovert, you can sometime be too garrulous for the common good.

I'm conscious of the dangers but have learned over my career that it is too easy just to get rid of the toxic teammate. My instinct is to give that individual more responsibility, a chance to atone. Sure, they will have to show signs of change at some point but give them time to work through their issues.

In the same way that we should kill the idea of the unicorn leader who will magically improve outcomes, we should not blame our organization's failings on one person. It's too easy to demonize a prickly individual. Remember why you employed them in the first place, and give them a chance to shine.

Build Your Team, Brick by Brick

Communication is paramount in a successful team. Everyone went after Cristiano Ronaldo in a million ways when he gave an incendiary interview to Piers Morgan criticizing Manchester United FC, which led to his mutual release from the club on the eve of his captaining Portugal in his fifth World Cup in Qatar.

I tended to agree with Roy Keane during what was an impassioned, interminable debate about how Ronaldo and Manchester United had reached that point. He condemned

Ronaldo's most vociferous critics as "idiots," an intervention that begged several central questions. What was the communication like between manager and player? Did Ronaldo have clarity about his role? Did he clearly accept that role? As leaders we have to be careful about the implementation of our authority.

It's easy to say, "I'm in charge. I've got more power than you." I am not saying that Ronaldo did not deserve to be dropped for refusing to go on to the pitch as a late substitute with the game already decided, but what had happened for things to reach that point?

It is easy to say he was out of order, but outsiders have no idea of what actually went down. It's possible the club may have wanted to make an example of him. A relatively new manager had the right to act on a fundamental matter of principle. Yet something tells me that in those circumstances internal communication cannot have been ideal.

Muhammad Ali famously observed, "The fight is won or lost far away from witnesses—in the mind, behind the lines, in the gym, and out there on the road, long before I dance under those lights." I fully believe more major titles are won in the dressing room than many realize.

In fact, I will go further. The dressing room is always the place in which they are won. To give a recent example, Manchester City were the better team in the 2022 Women's FA Cup final at Wembley. But there was no doubt in my mind that we were going to win.

Why? Because I know my locker room. I know the work we do. I know who we are. I know how we understand each other. I know what we do to strengthen our relationships. I know why we prevail, and how we come through really tough times.

Sure enough, we won 3–2 after extra time, despite the blow of conceding an equalizer that tied the match in the last minute of normal time.

That's why, in the early stages of my eight-week recuperation in October 2022, following my hysterectomy, I was sitting on the sofa at home, watching TV and screaming, "I fucking love this team" down my mobile to my staff on the bench in France. I never said it was pretty, but thanks to Millie Bright's first-half goal we became the first team to beat Paris Saint-Germain FC in their home stadium since 2015. I was so proud because I knew how hard Chelsea had worked. More importantly, they appreciated the work they had put in, on and off the pitch.

Achievements like that are rarely accidental. They are orchestrated, not organic. People talk about our amazing team spirit. That doesn't appear with a magician's flourish out of nowhere. It is built brick by brick.

When I look at the Premier League and the men's game, I see similar traits in the team being built at Arsenal. People talk about Mikel Arteta's intensity without appreciating the integrity of his approach. He has drilled the importance of collective culture into a relatively young group.

Culture is a composite of consistent actions. It involves constant reinforcement of certain behaviors and the expectation of meeting rigorous personal and professional standards. At Chelsea, our collective culture included me, the coaching team, support staff, and everyone from the team doctor to the groundsman. We all watched each other, expecting the best of one another. Accountability is critical.

I am in a relentless profession and get absolutely no rest. That's why I have certain rules I follow rigorously. First and foremost, I protect my self-confidence. That's vital, since I know there will be occasions when it seems the entire outside world is criticizing my decisions. For heaven's sake, even my family are critical of my coaching from time to time.

I have learned through experience to put the right mechanisms in place. When I doubt myself and begin to feel the gnawing pangs of anxiety, I shut myself away from things: I read nothing external related to my work. I do things I know make me happy, such as playing with my son Harry. In that way, I raise my spirits.

I don't complicate things. I stick to my fundamentals. Such self-preservation is a priority in the immediate aftermath of defeat because it can be overwhelming. Normally, when we have a midweek match, it's followed by two days of postgame analysis with trusted people. I can become highly emotional with certain aspects of performance and I need to temper those feelings and work through them before I might say things I will regret.

So, I hear you say, let's put this to the test. What are the qualities I look for in a good recruit? I am glad you asked that. Here are my seven values. I'll leave it to you to decide whether they are magnificent.

1. Primarily, I look for good team players. They recognize that some people around them will struggle. They are ready to respond by telling them they are appreciated and acknowledged. They unhesitatingly take up the slack.
2. Hard work and determination are at the heart of everything we do. I go back to what I was taught by my father. We cannot afford to be off by 1 percent if we want to be winners.

3. Honesty is another core value. You cannot manage people and processes without it. You have to look inward and outward without avoiding the truth. You need to be able to give and take feedback without rancor. Endear yourself to others by being genuine.

4. Humility goes hand in hand with honesty. I want my players and staff to come across as good people. I ask them to clean up after themselves. When members of the public approach them, I expect them to be uniformly polite. It costs nothing to be considerate.

5. A growth mindset is essential. Since that is a bit of a buzzword, I had better explain what I mean. I'm not looking for the next Einstein, but I am seeking someone who is committed to developing their talent and natural intelligence. That requires recognition that setbacks are an essential element of the learning process.

6. Diversity is key, even if it is difficult to detect in the over-regimented world of British sport. I do not want everyone to act and think in the same way. I value logical thinkers, but I've also got my eye out for someone with initiative and imagination, a leader rather than a follower.

7. Finally, trust is critical. It is an honor that must be earned. It offers security and reassurance. It rewards integrity and character. It is something that money cannot buy and fame cannot ensure. It's the hard currency of leadership.

Leaders have to be big enough to take the blame, and brave enough to question themselves. For all the talk about marginal gains—most often, in our case, involving the quality of our sports science or our analysis—effective management is about recognizing how people work as a unit. If the human interaction in your organization is flawed, the rest is irrelevant.

To summarize,

- discover what drives your team.
- encourage conflict resolution.
- build your team, brick by brick.

Chapter 4

What Is Leadership?

Good question.

For some, it involves delving into a lucky bag of inspirational quotes from excellent orators and trying to find a personal fit. For others, it requires the comfort blanket of a plan that worked for someone else in the same field.

All leaders scavenge bits and pieces. There's nothing wrong with that, but for me the essence of leadership is understanding your team and how your organization works. It depends on the application of interlocking virtues, the way people in our club, company, or department conduct themselves with our values and our collective goals. It means knowing what to do, when to do it, and why you do it.

It doesn't matter whether you are managing an office, running a production line, or coaching an elite sports team. Your primary role is to facilitate, to project manage. I see myself as a head contractor.

I'm building a house to the highest specifications, knowing the ground can shift suddenly beneath my feet. The job is fraught with daily difficulty. I have to synchronize a diverse group of highly skilled workers. I must recognize and weed out the coasters who cut corners. Principles are my foundation stones.

I oversee the architectural plans. They must be accurate, but they are not sacrosanct. They can be amended, subtly, if the need arises. There are so many different challenges, and some of them you simply don't see coming. Your response in real time is the key to keeping everyone moving in the right direction. People often say that's easier done with experience, without really defining what experience is.

Learn from Failure

I believe experience refers to wisdom, which is accumulated through failure. Experience is how we overcome the curve balls thrown in our path that develop our dexterity and durability as leaders. Yet I see very few individuals and organizations put those lessons into effective use. That doesn't signal a lack of commitment, but rather more of a confusion about the nature of the task.

Leadership is draining. You have to constantly listen well, communicate clearly, and reflect wisely. You must have a deep understanding of the human condition and be hyperaware of what makes people tick. Assume nothing. The range of motivational factors within your workforce is surprisingly wide. Age is an element that can creep up on you. Broadly speaking, I coach twentysomethings. Our social and cultural reference points are different. My understanding of them must shift constantly as I grow older and the world around us changes.

In my business, iconic players from a previous generation lose their relevance startlingly fast. No disrespect intended, and I realize this will be treated as heresy on Merseyside, but the vast majority of today's kids would not have a clue who Kenny Dalglish is. It's my job to bridge the generations and find more timely examples of excellence to expand upon. I can do that while remaining true to old school values because when it comes to teaching and learning there are eternal truths. To give an example, I live by the motto, "Stand, and live it every day." It may not be fashionable, but it works for me.

Everyday examples make the best points. For instance, why do most people commit speeding offenses? Because they are running late or trying to get somewhere in a hurry? You'd think so, but most of the time it's because they lose concentration.

They're on a familiar route, on autopilot. (I should know. I got my speeding tickets on the road I use every day.) But when you are on a new road, in a different environment with fresh landmarks, you don't make the same mistakes. In life there is always more than one path to take, and it's my job to direct my people on different routes. It's a simple premise: if you want a different result next time, take a different road. If your work-shops or team-building exercises are generating the same stale responses, try a new format or environment.

Become a Mentor

Many of us were lucky to have a mentor at school or in our community, maybe a youth worker or a favorite teacher who helped us to figure out our path in life. It is a fair bet that there are people on your team who now look to you for guidance. Taking an interest in what drives them is the job of the leader.

I consciously try to cultivate a cocoon of acceptance and assistance. In that sense, as I have already mentioned, coaching is a professional form of parenting. In its basic form, coaching is an exercise in trial and error. Like parenthood, no one really knows if they are doing it well. Not to put too fine a point on it, but for most of the time no one's got a bloody clue what's going on. They're just hoping for the best. My job involves the development of values, habits, and boundaries. Like a parent, I'm there to turn players into passable adults. Players can hate on their coach in the same way a child falls out with their mum or dad, but they will still turn to them in moments of personal crisis.

Simplicity is best. Humanity is all. I vividly remember listening to the *High Performance Podcast* in which Dutch coach Robin van Persie recounted watching his son Shaqueel deal with the frustrations of being left on the bench for Feyenoord in their Under-14 derby against AFC Ajax.

In the car on the way home, his son was moody and resentful, complaining about his coach and others in the team. Robin suggested he sounded like a loser, since he failed to recognize the possibility that he, too, was at fault. Winners, he explained, take control. They blame themselves and highlight where they can improve.

Shaqueel had a question to answer: Was he a winner or a loser? Robin explained his role as a father was to prepare him for life. He would understand and excuse his mistakes. His support was complete and unshakable. He would still love him, whatever decision he reached. Robin saw football was his son's passion, but it didn't ultimately matter to him if he emulated him by becoming a professional football player.

His observations struck a chord. Two days later, acting on a hunch, Robin went out of his way to watch his son train. He remembered, "My wife asked me why, but I wanted to see how he reacted. I am sitting there cold, hoodie on. I see this tiger, training, running, working. I said to myself, ah ok. He is fourteen and has realised he has to take control of his life."

Shaqueel is now sixteen and has signed his first professional contract with his father's first club. He is the top scorer for Feyenoord's Under-16 team and has been called up for the Netherlands's Under-17 team Robin has spent the last three years doing a variety of developmental coaching roles while studying for his coaching badges.

Robin, the Netherlands's record goal scorer, worked with Manchester United's young forwards and examined the club's coaching methodology at the invitation of manager Erik ten Hag just before the end of the World Cup break in December 2022. Robin returned early in the new year.

He has wisdom acquired over a stellar eighteen-year playing career to impart, but that insight into the ease and sensitivity of his parenting skills went a long way to convincing me he will mature into an outstanding coach. I'll be watching him keenly next season, when he begins his managerial career at Heerenveen, for whom he has signed a two-year contract as head coach.

If I worked every day to be popular, I would fail miserably. Being liked is not the same as being respected—but you've got to respect your own talents and abilities before others can. I know players will come to me when they hit rock bottom. People have complicated lives and everyone on your team or in your organization will have worries outside of work. As a leader, it's your job to remember that underperformance may be due to personal issues rather than a lack of engagement.

The really hard times tend to come out of the blue. Sometimes players have their first experience of death, involving a grandparent or occasionally a parent. They might have suffered their first relationship breakup. These are profound moments in their lives not to be scoffed at, downplayed, or ignored. It explains a lot about performance. A particular player might be homesick or dealing with dietary issues. There might be an eating disorder in the background or mental health challenges to contend with. Dealing with a crisis of confidence is difficult when you are used to adulation.

People watching from the outside have no idea what goes on beneath the surface. It stays out of the press because I consciously deflect attention. As a coach, you may know the real, deeply personal reason why someone is not playing well or not being selected, but it must never be divulged. That may mean taking uninformed criticism, but it is my job to protect my people. There is always a truth-telling moment when I ask my player, "How can I help you? What do you need?" A confession of vulnerability or weakness makes it so much easier for them.

It is daunting to reveal something private about yourself, but progression comes with self-awareness. It is a matter of trust. The player needs to have the confidence you will not judge them. That's the leader as a priest, the giver of absolution and understanding.

You might be judged as a coach on what we call the X's and O's, shorthand for the tactical game plan, but you're also a psychologist. There's no formal training in dealing with awkward conversations, but when someone comes to you and acknowledges she self-harms, there's the possibility that someone's life is in your hands.

In practice, you're a negotiator in addition to being a confidante, and how you manage such intimate information is crucial. That's one aspect of the loneliness of leadership; so much is down to you. I rarely have critical meetings on my own, and rely heavily on Paul Green, my general manager. We've worked together for eight years; he is my sounding board in the trickiest moments.

The doctor is available to be brought into the conversation. I'm not trained as a counselor, and I understand I might need the help of a clinical practitioner. I'm less inclined to fully involve psychologists because in my experience they tend to work in silos rather than in the multidisciplinary way I favor.

People don't always see what you are doing behind the scenes as a leader. No one knew the real reason Fran Kirby was unable to play for Chelsea FC for several months. She was diagnosed with a rare condition called pericarditis, an illness that causes inflammation to the fluid-filled sac around the heart.

Although Fran had been having dinner with two teammates, Maren Mjelde and Beth England, when she collapsed, we told the rest of the squad that she was suffering from a virus, in order not to spook them. She did not want to be a burden on her teammates. I was deliberately vague in addressing her absence with the media but tried to keep them onside by quietly asking them to back off, since she was a special talent who needed some breathing room.

Football was an irrelevance in this case. All I wanted was for Fran to be well. In my twenty-five years as a coach, I have never seen a player transform her life so profoundly. Fran has overcome despair and disruption. She has negotiated the emotional extremes of fear and joy. She has shown gratitude for everything football has given to her, but, above all, inspirational application in confronting her challenges.

In my mind's eye, I do not see Fran skipping around Wembley, having won the European Championship with England. I see a young woman weeping bitterly in my office after being sick during a premature return to training a fortnight after her original episode.

Inclusivity is the hallmark of intelligent leadership. During a recent international break, I made a point of inviting two players to all our staff meetings to give them greater insight.

I try to be proactive and relate to journalists on a human level. They also have high-pressure jobs and personal issues with which to contend. I worry about safeguarding and welfare issues. A younger, more naive coach might have been in trouble receiving a call as I did at ten o'clock one night from a player who was distraught because she felt she had been trapped by a reporter into talking about a sensitive personal issue concerning fat-shaming at a previous club.

I knew the fallout could easily trigger her propensity to tip back into damaging introspection and an eating disorder, and I promised to do all I could to get the media outlet to drop its story. They did so, after the delicacy of the player's background had been explained to them. Other newspaper editors might not have been so sympathetic, but on this occasion my reputation for being fair, candid, and considerate helped.

Football's relentless publicity machine creates convenient illusions. Prominent managers and coaches are overpraised and underappreciated as the media sees fit. We are more rounded figures than we are given credit for and lauded for things that are ultimately marginal. We love the image of the leader as a tyrant, intolerant of failure, when in reality most of us are social workers.

One of the most valuable skills in any leader is an appreciation of body language. You have to read the room quickly and understand how to steer the conversation. Is my player frustrated? Is she lacking confidence? Is she tired? She looks frazzled. Each player has individual tics, which give away underlying concerns.

I sometimes wish I could have a camera with me. You see them casting their eyes down. They can't focus. They don't know what to do. They don't know what to feel. That's why, when the group is around me, I tell them to look at me in the eye. I know I need to get them out of their own heads. Once they do that, I do the rest.

It's a complex, delicate process. One emerging player confided that she was suffering anxiety attacks. That sense of panic seeped into her play, and she was developing a reputation within the group as someone who couldn't handle the pressure of the biggest matches. She wanted to be trusted but, as I explained to her, that would be impossible if her teammates didn't know who she was. She was hiding. She had to be willing to give something of herself. I insisted that she should tell them of her struggles, because in doing so she would unleash the power of understanding.

She was afraid of being seen as weak, but I outlined the difference between weakness and vulnerability. She was terrified of addressing the group on her own, but instead of having me beside her in the dressing room, I sent her in with my two captains, Magda and Millie, because I knew their indication of faith in her would be much more powerful.

It was for the team to accept her as one of them. They went into a huddle, and she explained her struggles with her mental health. She talked about the days when it was hard to get out of bed, the nights when she agonized about not performing to her potential.

I learned later that, when she had poured out her heart, the team gathered around her and consumed her in a giant hug. They told her they had guessed that anyway, and that they were there for her. She felt the weight of the world lift off her shoulders.

My message, when I saw her afterward, was heartfelt. "Everyone knows who you are, and you can come into work every day knowing you don't have to hide from that. This is your safe space." Little by little, her season got better and better.

Some of her problem was down to a lack of belief, an insidious feeling of inadequacy. If you make a mistake in a match and you can't let it go, it can easily damage you as a player. You have to move on. That's why I teach athletes to think like goldfish, who, according to urban myth, have a three-second memory span.

OK, OK. I know that has been disproved scientifically. The little orange miracles apparently have a memory that stretches weeks, months, and even years. I call my players Nemos even though in the film *Finding Nemo* the principal character has a perfect memory, unlike his friend Dory, the Pacific blue tang fish.

Vulnerability is hard to deal with, and some need individual therapy to develop defense mechanisms. Others don't need formal management because they have learned greater self-sufficiency. The range of resilience I have seen as a coach is quite amazing.

I've had players whose parents have a history of addictions. Some have been abused in some way in earlier life. Others have had to come to terms with personal tragedy. I am so proud of one particular player who was operating at the top of her game because I know what she has been through in her life. I can't relate to some of the things she has endured, but I tell her to embrace every minute of her success. I feel connected to my players in so many different ways, because I know how influential certain guides and muses have been in my own life.

We work in a world of immediate, often brutal judgment. Since one of the hardest things in coaching is trying not to be too harsh or too hard when things go wrong, empathy is an essential element of modern leadership.

There's a bit of David Attenborough in all of us because we have to recognize the subspecies of individuals we must deal with. Any workplace contains sharks and snakes, who will do anything to survive. The T-Rexes, dinosaurs who are oblivious to the incoming meteorite, need watching for complacency. I love the cats, the ones who are deceptively serene, independent, and ruthless. The guide dogs are quiet and diligent leaders. The loyalty of lapdogs is inherently selfish. The meerkats are constantly seeking attention and looking for praise. The grizzly bears relish their menace.

Noticing these characteristics in people is a good first step in knowing how to deal with them. It's survival of the fittest. I have my quiet influencers who you'd think wouldn't hurt a fly, but by God do they know how to stay at the highest level. Their diligence is extraordinary.

Human chemistry makes watching a team fascinating when it is all going wrong. You see different character profiles emerge. Certain individuals come to the fore, while others shrink into the shadows. A leader must be a diplomat, looking beyond the now, assessing risk, accumulating knowledge, and developing nuance and subtlety. One of the problems with football is that too many people know only football; they lack a finer understanding of the way humans work. A good leader knows what makes people tick.

I also see an elite soldier's resourcefulness in leaders I admire. Their jobs involve constant preparation, conscious control, and perfect execution. There are times when you have to be ice cold. You train your brain to think clearly in action, even if your heart rate is pounding through your chest. When you've been triggered and your heart is banging like a drum, you need to be able to slow your breathing down quickly and allow your rational brain to take over.

Leaders should model the behaviors they want to see in their people. I aim to deliver bite-size chunks of common sense to my players. Practice your next move. Don't get caught up in the heat of the moment. Remember, your rivals are also seeking to improve continually. They are searching for the same edge, that elusive magical formula.

We can all sit around talking innovation until the cows come home, but certain rules apply. Teams get better the more they play together. That's basic stuff. Performance, on a daily basis, is driven by everyone, regardless of status.

My job within that structure is not to have all the answers and solutions. Rather, it is to facilitate a sufficiently coherent plan using everyone else's knowledge. With up to three games a week, I have to pull that together quickly and execute it succinctly.

There's limited time, maybe as little as a single training session on the grass and one fifteen-minute classroom session. I've had to become world class at public speaking, delivering messages that hook people rapidly and securely. Prepare assiduously. Be aware of your body language, relax, and control your breathing. Speak concisely, yet passionately. Above all, know your audience. Appealing to people's self-interest is key: I always make it clear to the players what is in it for them.

Practice Good Self-Care

I've learned to meditate, in real time. I'm mindful of my wellness, and meditation is a performance enhancer. I meditate with my staff before matches, but I have yet to persuade my players, no matter how many times I invite them and how effusively I describe the benefits.

My interest was stimulated by Phil Jackson, the celebrated basketball coach who won eleven NBA Championships with the Chicago Bulls and Los Angeles Lakers. He is a very spiritual guy. He inspired legendary players such as Michael Jordan, Kobe Bryant, and Shaquille O'Neal through a mixture of Native American philosophy, humanistic psychology, and Zen meditation.

When I came into Chelsea, I introduced Eva Woods as our women's health coach. Her role was to monitor my staff as well as my players. She introduced yoga and meditation into the program. We learned techniques that could be used individually, when we felt stress levels rising, but also operated in a group setting.

Michael Macintyre is my personal breath and meditation coach. He was instrumental in helping me through my pregnancy, and after Harry's birth helped to strengthen my diaphragm following the hysterectomy. He gets my mind and body in sync. He has also worked with my support team at Chelsea. We meditated before games in the hotel. Michael might be on a computer link while we lay on the floor. The session usually involved a half hour's concentration on our breathing, and another half hour honing relaxation techniques. The staff loved him; he has the soothing voice of an angel.

If you're not looking after yourself properly, things can fall apart at work. I'm really hard on myself. I'll talk things over with one of my assistants or maybe a mentor if I feel the need, but usually no one comes near me after a loss. My family gives me space. Just leave me alone. Let me walk Harry to school, take him to the park. Let me exercise, let me breathe, let me get myself clear.

Getting enough sleep is extra important if you have a demanding career. I used to find it difficult to sleep, but with Harry now, I'm knackered at the end of the day. I find myself going to bed earlier and earlier. I still wake up in the middle of the night, of course, especially in the build-up to big games. When I'm staring at the ceiling in the darkness, I know I need to quickly get as much out of my head as possible. I constantly try to remove doubt from my mind because it is natural to obsess about the possibility of losing. I've learned the importance of reminding myself there are things that I cannot control.

I have a notebook by the side of my bed where I scribble down random thoughts, which could range from the previous day's training session to past matchups, or notes on conversations to have with certain staff members. Once that brain dump has been completed, I can switch off.

Well, usually.

I confess to a far less desirable habit of 3:00 a.m. text messages to my coaching staff. I pride myself in having my finger on the pulse, and often send reminders of small issues we need to nail down while these are in my mind. I value my staff immensely, but it's fair to say I don't always get the tone right, or the time.

Denise, my long-term assistant coach, can be relied on to reply in kind while sensible souls are asleep: "You get world coach of the year. Now we've got to deal with your fat arse head fitting in the office." I told her I expected her to make the tea the next morning but, as we say in London, I was bang to rights. She knows me too well.

In a nutshell, the essence of good leadership is understanding your team and how your organization works. A great leader

- learns from failure.
- becomes a mentor.
- practices good self-care.

Chapter 5

Only Women Bleed

I come from a place of suffering.

I am leaning heavily against a perimeter wall near the dugout where the managers, coaches, and substitutes sit, praying I don't pass out when the cameras are trained on me. I would usually be buzzing around my technical area, a loud, hyperactive figure drawn magnetically to the touchline.

On this particular day, September 18, 2022, during the first Super League game of a new season at Prenton Park, adopted home of Liverpool's women's team, I am lost in private agony. I had been unwell in the team hotel beforehand, which hadn't been unusual for far too long. I just learned to cope.

Judging by the reaction of Liverpool's Matt Beard, my opposite number, the pretense of normality was unconvincing. "Are you all right?" he asked when we met in the tunnel beforehand. His concern triggered a rare confession. "I don't want to go out there," I told him. "I don't feel very well."

He was lovely about it, organizing a bed for me in a quiet area close to the dressing rooms, but the brain fog didn't lift. I'm usually quick to make decisions but spent the entire second half thinking *we need a goal* without doing anything about it.

71

Denise Reddy has known me since 2008, when we began working together for the Chicago Red Stars. She told me later that all she could think of was why isn't Emma on her feet? We lost, 2–1, and all I could think of was *I'm going to lose more than this game if I'm not careful.*

I hid my fears when I addressed players and staff in the traditional postmatch huddle. "I'm so confident of our response to this," I told them. "I know exactly who we are. We know who we are. Look after each other this week, because if the criticism comes in, we've got it."

That took the last of my energy. I nearly fainted. I had reached the point where my body had stopped fighting. I couldn't hide my pain any longer. The next time I spoke to the team, two days later, I broke the news that I needed an emergency hysterectomy. There was no other choice.

I help those players win football matches. We collected sixteen trophies in my time at Chelsea FC. It's what I do for a living, but hopefully not what defines me. Football management involves projecting a strange mixture of serenity and urgency. It's supposed to signal certainty and authority.

This medical emergency was raw, elemental. Human. I became extremely upset as waves of sadness, pride, guilt, and fear washed over me. I had been distant, almost antisocial during preseason preparations, when I took a step back and allowed Denise and Tanya Oxtoby, another of my coaches, to develop their roles.

I felt bad about my inner isolation. In my moment of surrender, I was overwhelmed by the tenderness and kindness of the young women I care so much for. We hugged and cried together as a group. Trying hard to remain rational in the most emotional of circumstances, I knew then they would be strong for me.

Alex Laurence, my gynecologist, told me the five-and-a-half-hour operation, complicated by chronic endometriosis, was the most difficult surgical procedure she had performed in her career. "I don't know how you lived with it," she said. I replied, "I didn't know I had it."

Sally Harris, the other amazing doctor responsible for my care, was the first to recognize the extent of my distress. She suggested I would have had a heart attack, fueled by stress, within five years had I continued to struggle on in survival mode.

One of the responsibilities of leadership is using the platform it provides for the common good. I had been increasingly vocal about the insidious nature of endometriosis, which affects around one in ten women in the UK, and yet it takes on average between eight and ten years to diagnose. It is an ovarian condition that creates adhesions that strangle internal organs and can spread to the lungs and even the brain.

I had spoken about insufferably painful periods, chronic pain in the back and pelvis, bloating, and the gnawing dread of infertility. My initial anger has eased into gratitude for my recovery, but it is still my business to make it personal.

I am upset for Margaret, one of many women who emailed me. We are the same age, forty-six, and we both had deep infiltration endometriosis, the most acute stage of the disease. My operation revealed adhesions around my bowel, diaphragm, and abdominal wall.

I am upset for the twenty-five-year-old, curled up in bed, suffering profoundly. Her pain is constant, physical, and mental. She is a young woman who yearns for a child and cannot bear the consequences of the solution to her problems, the removal of her womb.

I am upset for the nineteen-year-old, who I can see enduring in unnecessary ignorance. She is clearly suffering from endometriosis or polycystic ovaries, and yet cannot get the help she needs and deserves as a basic right.

I am angry because these women do not lack curiosity. I want to cry for them because I empathize with them and identify with what they are going through.

They are sold short on basic gynecological care. It can take up to two years to see a gynecologist in Britain, depending on where you live. According to NHS England Data Resources, in 2022, 38,231 women waited for more than a year to see a gynecologist.

I have family in the medical profession and my understanding is that there are enough trained gynecologists but most leave the system because there is not enough investment in women's health. There are not enough jobs for these doctors to occupy in a disintegrating system.

Women have little option but to self-diagnose. General practitioners are undertrained in this area. Costs of diagnosis are deemed prohibitive because it involves the expense of vaginal ultrasound and MRI scans. If this was a male disease a cure would have already been found because it is so debilitating. It is similar to an autoimmune disease, like multiple sclerosis, triggering an imbalance in the immune system. No one really understands its causes and if it is hereditary. I suffered from a very early age and was never given an insight into my reproductive life cycle as a woman.

It is only now I have a better understanding of the links from puberty to menopause. It is only now, feeling like a completely different human being, that I realize just how ill I was. I have been a football manager a long time and understand the stresses of the role, but I was continually exhausted. I would switch my brain on to do my job to the best of my ability and crash when I came home.

I feel like I've been living behind frosted glass. Everything was dysfunctional. My pain levels were profound. I had been unable to take a deep breath or exhale properly for four years. I have had a bladder infection for the same length of time, caused by damage I was completely unaware of. I convinced myself it was absolutely normal to be peeing every forty-five minutes or so.

I became used to dismissive, so-called explanations: "Oh, you've got a stressful job . . . It's your periods . . . You're not getting enough sleep . . . You're a new mum. . . ." One gynecologist said I had a hernia when it was in fact an endometrial mass.

I consider myself reasonably well read, but the knowledge gap is frightening. I had a laparoscopy (keyhole surgery) in 2015 in an attempt to get well around the time when we won our first double at Chelsea. I didn't know that having an in vitro fertilization treatment, and subsequently giving birth to my son Harry, fueled endometriosis. I wasn't told that being in high hormone stages, when estrogen and progesterone levels are elevated, and then having a C-section intensified the adhesions and scarring in my body.

I was frustrated because I had a very healthy lifestyle. I rarely drink and I don't smoke. I had given up things such as dairy products and gluten. I had taken up meditation, which I used to try and get back to sleep during those endless, uncomfortable nights when my joints stiffened.

Yet the disease was driving up my levels of cortisol, the body's primary stress hormone. This resulted in more extensive inflammation and water retention. I felt swollen everywhere. I thought I had digestive issues, because I was living with the extremes of diarrhea and constipation. I now know my bowel was being choked.

The irony is that during that time my public profile soared as women's football entered the mainstream sporting consciousness. It is hard to look at myself in photographs of Chelsea celebrating the double—winning Britain's top tier division and a club's primary domestic Cup competition in the same season—in 2018, 2021, and 2022. When the cameraman captured me lifting Harry and the Cup on the pitch, all I see is the illness in me. Football management is such an all-consuming profession that we do not look after ourselves as well as we should, but its insecure nature means we identify strongly with one another. Once my condition became public, my peers rallied around.

Sir Alex Ferguson was one of the first to call. We had been sitting together at a League Managers Association awards dinner when Dr. Sally Harris, who has played a fundamental role in caring for many others in our profession, told me, presciently, "I'll be seeing you soon. You do so much to help others and it is my job to help you."

Pep Guardiola and Jurgen Klopp sent me long messages, expressing deeply felt emotions. Graham Potter and David Moyes did the same. They have mothers, wives, sisters, and daughters. Their empathy was natural, and unforced.

As a coach and leader of women players and staff at Chelsea, I developed a sensitivity to specific health issues. Some of my players had regular periods, and they are fine, without underestimating the debilitating pain many women suffer for a couple of days each month. Others had elongated cycles, the reasons for which are not simple and can be very different. It can range from a lack of nutrients, overtraining, irregular hormonal health, or the result of being on the contraceptive pill.

I'm proud that in 2020 we became the first club to use a specialist tracking app to tailor training around players' menstrual cycles. We incorporate possible effects such as slow reaction times and low serotonin levels into our performance planning. These feed into our holistic management approach.

Football offers us a platform to address ignorance. England captain Leah Williamson powerfully and publicly acknowledged her fears that endometriosis, which left her crippled with pain, would sabotage her performances in the UEFA European Championship. Beth England, who won the PFA Women's Players' Player of the Year Award in 2020 and was featured in that triumphant England squad, has also opened up about her struggle with endometriosis. She has undergone two operations. It has been so acute at times that she has been forced to abandon training sessions. Although she moved from Chelsea to Tottenham, we are sisters from different generations, bonded by our pain.

There is no embarrassment among male members of my staff, whose awareness of intimate medical details informs their work. As for my more experienced female coaches, many of whom are coming to terms with the idiosyncrasies of the perimenopause, we share war stories like old soldiers.

I've often been out on the training pitch with Denise, overseeing a passage of play or a specific drill, while whispering to her, "I'm in agony. My back is killing me, and my knees are hurting." She'll give me that look of sad solidarity and confide, "My brain's not here today, and my skin is itching."

There are more than thirty symptoms of menopause, and before we know it we're going back and forth with a litany of complaints. We're doing our job, while asking ourselves, "Is it natural to feel like this?"

One of the first maxims of good leadership is the importance of self-care and to listen to what your body is telling you. You can't effectively care for others unless you're looking after yourself. In that spirit, I've come to appreciate the campaigning work of two strong, high-profile women. If I can be half as effective as them, it will mean as much to me as the medals that dangle over the central island in my open-plan kitchen at home.

We owe so much to Davina McCall for the work she has done on her menopause manifesto. As she says, in a contribution to the Menopause Charity website, "I used to think that menopause was an age thing and now I realise it's a woman thing. For far too long, there's been a shroud of embarrassment, shame, and fear around this topic, and this is where it stops."

She was forty-four and, in her own words, felt as if she was losing it. The traditional symptom, hot flushes, was accompanied by depression and mental fog. Now, through her support of the Menopause Charity—which is not sponsored by any pharmaceutical companies—she is helping thousands of women to access honest and helpful advice.

Vicky McClure, the BAFTA-winning actress, is enabling people to connect the dots between the menopause and dementia. The cognitive decline that can happen in women during this time of life is so weighty, yet the need for greater research and understanding is often blithely dismissed.

Menopausal brain fog and the early stages of Alzheimer's disease share certain symptoms. Hormone replacement therapy (HRT) in perimenopause can slow cognitive decline and protect against neurodegenerative disease.

Having lived in the public eye, one thing Vicky and I share is an understanding of how modern media works, and the power of a well-planned strategic challenge to authority. I was particularly struck by one video featuring Vicky, who has raised the profile of the annual Memory Walks that raise millions of dollars for the Alzheimer's Society charity.

In the video she speaks directly to the camera, asking MPs to imagine trading their life in the political arena with that of an unpaid carer for someone with dementia. She called on them to mend the broken social care system, and confronted their consciences by outlining the exhausting physical, emotional, and financial problems faced by thousands of affected families.

I realize I have a somewhat unusual story to tell, and after seeing the examples set by Davina and Vicky, I believe I have a responsibility beyond the football pitch. Instead of putting out the usual cautious, almost coy, statement that I'd had a "surgical procedure," I insisted on it mentioning the emergency nature of my hysterectomy, and the underlying reasons for it.

Even though that statement wasn't for me, it was about me. Its openness was designed to shed a glimmer of light in the direction of the poor women who are out there suffering. They are not alone. I have a responsibility to their health, and to question why it takes so long to see a gynecologist.

So many women and their partners have written to me, worrying about the length of time it takes to diagnose endometriosis, and arrange hysterectomies, if required. I couldn't believe how little support there is and how much unnecessary pain is being caused.

I am a keen student of social and political history, and, like many coaches, I place great importance on self-education. Reading a study of Victorian England, I learned that by 1900 the average life expectancy for a woman was fifty years. Living standards in the late nineteenth century rose substantially. Food was more nourishing. Public health was better, due to clean water and an improved sewage system.

Yet sometimes age is not just a number. A thought struck me. Fifty years old is regarded as the typical age at which menopause leaves the body without the hormones that fuel it. Women struggle to function effectively without estrogen, which declines as we get older. In a woman of age fifty, estrogen levels are at half the peak usually experienced in their mid- to late twenties.

Estrogen is important because it lubricates our joints and protects our brain cells. As my doctor calls it, the "liquid gold" isn't there. This is what we are referring to when talking as women of a certain age about mental fog. It dulls our senses, derails our train of thought, and leaves us struggling to complete simple sentences.

I couldn't have HRT because it would have aggravated my endometriosis. That has changed fundamentally, following my operation. Eventually, extreme fatigue will become a thing of the past. My brain feels alive again.

A Women's Health Initiative study in 2002 found that HRT increased the level of risk of heart disease and breast cancer. However, since then, safer versions of the treatment have been developed.

Dr. Sarah McKay is the neurologist who has taught me so much about how our minds and brains are shaped by our genes, hormones, life experiences, belief systems, society, and culture. She told me that if you take HRT, you have a 4 in 1000 chance of getting breast cancer within a given year. If you are not taking HRT, there is a 3 in 1000 chance of getting breast cancer.

HRT is available over the counter, if you can afford it and have taken the precaution of appropriate advice regarding it. If you are relying on the UK's National Health Service, at a time when doctor appointments are difficult to come by, you enter a postcode lottery. That cannot be right.

I am not saying there aren't stringent ways to deal with the problem organically. Plant-based diets, the consumption of foods rich in calcium and vitamin D, and the avoidance of refined sugars and processed food help relieve menopause symptoms. But a holistic approach needs to be carefully orchestrated, and it can be complex and expensive.

I have been on a profound journey trying to piece all of this together. As women, we are taught the three basics of our reproductive cycle: the trauma of the onset of periods in adolescence, the opportunity and challenge of giving birth, and the inevitability of the menopause.

But what about the other connections? Worldwide, women with Alzheimer's disease, the most common form of dementia, outnumber men two to one. Scans reveal that the rate at which cells are dying in the brain is faster in women than in men. In the US, women began to be included in clinical trials for dementia in 1986, but this was not enshrined in law until 1993.

Things are changing, slowly. A 2021 study of nearly 400,000 women found that HRT drugs reduced the risk of diseases that cause dementia, and a 2023 study showed that HRT had more cognitive benefits for women at greater risk of developing it. But, still, not enough questions are being asked. Why do we tolerate the political choice not to invest in women's health? As leaders, it is our job to protect our people. Get on that soapbox and shout. You may be surprised how far your voice will carry.

Some points to remember:

- Women are impacted by their menstrual cycle and by menopause, and both can adversely affect attendance and performance.
- I would recommend any woman to use a menstrual cycle tracking app.
- As a leader, it is your job to protect your people.

Chapter 6

Don't Laminate It. Live It.

Worthy books are written on the concept of values-based leadership. Word-salad presentations are performed every day in businesses across the land with corporate correctness. Positions are taken, stances are struck, and promises are made. It's common sense transformed into theater. Don't get me wrong. I appreciate the significance of a clearly expressed set of personal and professional standards. They should feed into the decision-making process and encourage an emotional connection within your group.

But . . . there's always a "but," isn't there?

In far too many cases, these books and presentations are a crock of shit. It's a world of laminated mission statements that sit on the organization's walls and make precious little sense because they are words without actions. The principles expressed are undeniably important, but the process is worthless because it is largely virtue-signaling.

I'm all about bringing values in a culture to life. In my opinion, that doesn't happen enough. That exposes me, as a leader, to the obvious retort: Well, what did you do about it at Chelsea then? Our staff and players sat down as a team and provided the answer, on my behalf.

Chelsea has six core organizational values:

1. We are here to win
2. Be brave
3. Do the right thing
4. Play my part
5. Many teams, one club
6. Proud to be Chelsea

The most important of those values is the first. It is a stark, simple expression of intent. It is also the bridge to the five values that follow it. It is easy to talk about the shared objective of winning and success, but what processes make those words meaningful? What does it entail, in terms of daily commitment? What does it look like? How driven are we to be the best? Do we truly, deeply appreciate what goes into being a top performer, in any business, let alone something as hyperdriven as professional football at an elite level?

It goes beyond natural talent. Always. It doesn't matter whether you are a prolific free-kick taker like David Beckham, or a global phenomenon like Cristiano Ronaldo attempting to defy the aging process at thirty-seven. It is all consuming. We see Beckham, the icon, rather than the player who spent endless hours perfecting his art. We don't see Ronaldo, minutes after winning the Champions League final, cajoling his teammates and letting them know that they had to repeat the following season.

At the 2022 World Cup in Qatar, and during Ronaldo's brief and unfulfilling return to Manchester United we witnessed an extreme but entirely human response to the frustration of being unable, at age thirty-seven, to do what he did at age twenty-seven. He yearned to be seventeen years old, with his football life ahead of him. Being the best isn't physical. It's emotional. It's spiritual. It becomes who you are, for better or for worse.

How did we respond as a group to Chelsea's six organizational values? We realized these overarching club values had to be broken down further, and aimed for the following:

1. Clear focus
2. Relentless pursuit of excellence
3. Reflect and review for improved future performance
4. Constantly strive to improve
5. Celebrate our success
6. Enjoy the journey

Statements of the bloody obvious? You'd think so. But here's why I think they're fundamental, individually and collectively. Having been laid out by the team, we work on them every week. More often than not, this involves concentrating on one component.

Suppose we decide to focus on the notion of reflection and reviewing. This cannot be a one-way process. Over my last couple of years at Chelsea, I got the players to reflect and review my performance and that of the entire department. It took some time to settle in to this because some of my staff were defensive and resistant to such scrutiny, but gradually it became habitual.

We surveyed the entire environment. What about our training week? Did we do well? What can we improve on? Was the right balance struck between preparing the starting eleven and ensuring the finishers, our substitutes, were able to make an impact? It had tangible, practical benefits.

The players felt one of the reasons we lost at Liverpool at the start of the 2022–2023 season was that the bus left the hotel twenty minutes late. It disrupted their rhythm and affected the mood. OK, then, how can we break down the logistics to avoid something similar happening again?

Let's count the steps from the meeting room to the bus. How many elevators are in operation to allow forty people to get down to the ground floor as soon as possible? Do we have to factor in the possibility of being in an underground garage? Will that add extra time when leaving for the match?

My job is to make sure the players have no excuses. Everyone gets more comfortable because of such forward thinking. People don't carry grievances into little rooms. If they feel something is not right, they can get it off their chests.

How are we going to break new ground? Suggestions anyone? Are there examples to follow? Other fields to explore? Is everybody really open to making that sort of commitment? Are we authentic about who we are, and what we want to be?

You'd be surprised how many will respond to the constant challenges if the atmosphere is right. Football clubs are notoriously impersonal places with a silo mentality, but we found ourselves being drawn toward other areas of the organization. I call it being the coach of the little big things. We might be part of a globally recognized institution, whether it's Chelsea or US Soccer, but the impact we can make goes beyond what we achieve on the pitch.

To give an example, groups of my players and staff at Chelsea would regularly meet with our marketing and commercial teams. Not everyone in the squad was interested, but some had a passion for those areas of activity. Helping to drive the direction of those departments is surprisingly personal, since the work they do contributes to the way our fans and the wider public perceived us.

It reinforces what we stood for as a club. We are all in it together. That is an easy phrase to trot out and can invite cynicism since we all know professional sport at the highest level is ruthlessly competitive and underpinned by self-interest.

We're not a Girl Guides troop, but we can prove we care. (Incidentally, can you imagine me as Brown Owl, the adult leader? The mind boggles.) Our values are layered, so their influence is widened, and their meaning is reinforced. Whatever the industry, people have to cooperate with colleagues to maximize their own advancement.

Here is another subset of six aims, related to the overarching organizational value of being brave that we adopted:

1. Be brave
2. Be decisive whatever the challenge
3. Innovate
4. Be the best version of yourself
5. Be honest with the team
6. Trust each other and be open with feedback

Trust and openness are key areas in my view. Over time, it becomes relatively easy to take the emotional temperature of a dressing room. Deep down, we know when something is festering. That's why we do a lot of work with what we refer to as the elephant in the room.

We talk a lot about avoiding cliques. I insist on players and staff constantly changing tables at lunchtime. I don't want them sitting with their mates every day, staking out their territory. If I spot cliques developing among the players, I'll jump on it. Tight friendship groups can restrict working relationships.

Let's say we have spotted two players habitually drifting off into a corner and chatting conspiratorially. While these two might be discussing their personal lives, they need to be aware of how it might be perceived. On the other hand, if they are having a particularly hard time, then their teammates need to know if they can help and how. Cliquey behavior needs to be confronted quickly, and it would be regularly called out in our weekly reflection sessions.

"Listen," I might say. "Being honest with the team is something we have committed to, but we are not doing it if we have players detaching themselves from the group and muttering among themselves. If you think you know a better way, speak out. If you don't understand, ask."

My players also know they have the go-ahead to take the initiative if they see standards being threatened. That's empowerment. That's a public invitation to contribute. That's what being a good teammate is all about.

Involve your team in actively breaking down these values and invite them to come up with ways they can be applied. The idea is to avoid empty sloganeering and corporate speak, to elevate great ideas into effective actions. We win and lose as a team. I know that is another easy, suspiciously empty phrase, so let's dive deeper into what that means.

After a defeat, the dressing room is a dangerous, volatile place. It's where pressure valves burst, bad smells linger. A player pegged for a mistake can easily become defensive: "I didn't fucking know what I was meant to be doing. No one told me." This is the time to stress that the coaching team and the playing group are indivisible. This is not a them-and-us situation. We are all interconnected, united around a common cause. To be consistent, I'd ask the complaining player to put herself in the coaching team's shoes when hearing this feedback.

The Why Can Be More Important Than the Who

Our job as coaches is to provide clarity on the game plan and detailed insight into individual roles and responsibilities. We're not perfect, so occasionally this information can be indistinct. It is the job of anyone who doesn't understand what is required of them to seek confirmation—just as teachers encourage students to ask for help if they haven't understood the instructions.

To give a recent example of a postmatch review, usually undertaken the following day, one of my players, a young defender, conspicuously failed to carry out her assigned area of the game plan. To be blunt, she went rogue, ignoring agreed expectations of how she would perform. This wasn't about apportioning blame and belittling an individual in front of her peers. It is possible to discuss difficulties without being insulting or intimidating. Our job, as leaders in such circumstances, was to determine why her lapse occurred.

How can we help to ensure it doesn't happen again? Never underestimate the power of repetition. She will be given regular reminders that she should let us know if she doesn't understand the demands placed on her. She should ask for guidance. That's not singling her out. It's a commitment from me to her that I will do all I can to help her improve.

Everyone has setbacks. If players hold themselves accountable, they also have the right to call us out, at the right time and in the right manner. Complaints can be constructive. Rather than muttering loosely away from disciplines of the review process about the specifics of our preparation, I try to encourage players to approach me directly with their suggestions. That's part of who we are.

It was not an overnight success story. We took years to get to the point when this worked for everyone. It involved the basics of trust and respect. As I've already mentioned, I'm seeking to avoid the passive-aggressive behavior that destroys the type of culture we are attempting to sustain. It generates a malign energy that is difficult to quantify. People expect you to read the nonverbal clues and signs of latent anger that suggest something is brewing while remaining reluctant to address their issues directly. Poor body language can highlight flaws in team culture. Performances can suggest certain individuals haven't bought into their roles or into the game plan.

A football club, like any workplace, is shaped by bad examples, just as surely as it is influenced by enlightened ones. It's not as simple as putting talented people together and expecting a dynamic team to emerge. You have to work very hard on creating a successful team. One of my best messages leaves little room for misunderstanding: "Your attitude is contagious. So pick the right one. . . ."

One of the big challenges for a leader is how to get the best out of the difficult individual with the huge talent and the sunny employee who produces average work. These people should be able to learn from each other, but how?

We intentionally use lots of happy visuals in team meetings to illustrate our aims. We're seeking to accentuate the positive and call out the thoughtlessly negative in an understated yet effective manner. I occasionally ask the club photographers to take pictures of really poor body language on the pitch. That might seem a bit Big Brotherish, but the world might be watching.

I've a thing about people yawning. Why? Tell me, what happens when someone yawns? Everyone around them also yawns. Energy levels drop. The air goes out of the room. The atmosphere changes. That creative edge is lost. It's the same when the Eeyores mooch around the place talking about having a shit day. That attitude is a product of lazy thinking and can rub off on others.

The projection of negative energy happens in every workplace, and at Chelsea we challenged it at every opportunity. If a player has genuine concerns about their performance, or they've had seriously bad news, terrible media feedback, or are dealing with a significant life challenge, my door is always open. I'd rather give the player some space to off-load, to see how I can best support them, than have them suffer in silence.

If you want to raise energy levels in your department or place of work, then focus on those who are passive by nature. This is their culture, too. Encourage them to live it. They may feel overshadowed by the extroverts who get all the attention and feel unable to vocalize their observations. If your organization's values are more than just a whiteboard of smiley faces, the quietest members of your team should feel included.

Staff and players choose to make our values relevant by making sure they are adhered to. Here's another small example of the buy-in that, over time, becomes second nature to all of us. I was exchanging texts with Millie Bright, the England defender who is one of my team leaders, the day after a match during my convalescence. I told her it was agony watching the game. Without allowing me to expand, she replied, "It is agony, if we don't carry out the game plan."

Millie amplified her point in the subsequent review meeting when the players led discussions. They drilled down into the problems and assumed ownership of the solution. In short, they didn't need me to be involved. They were on autopilot, in a good way.

Don't get me wrong, I challenge them all the time, and I want them to reciprocate by challenging me. Together, we will keep evolving. We will continue to improve. Simplicity will be our ally. We will embrace and develop progressive behavior. Our expectations of one another will be clear. We will mirror our culture.

It's not about individuals. Teams win trophies. If dear old menopausal Emma and Denise can contribute, then brilliant. If players can find something deeper within themselves to make others around them more productive, then so much the better.

People leap to conclusions about successful teams. They look at the trophies and the trinkets, and automatically assume they are won because we have the best players and the most money. If only it was that straightforward.

Every now and again I feel a need to reinforce the reality of what we have signed up to. I have become a stickler for punctuality. That starts with my coaches. If the team meeting convenes at 10:45 a.m., I won't have someone firing up their laptop at 10:47. I know how much that is going to piss the players off. It should. Why are we asking them to be on time, if we can't be? That's a basic sign of disrespect. It sends a terrible message that your time is more precious than other people's.

Almost everyone in performance sport can recite the story of Vince Lombardi, the iconic National Football League coach, who expected his players to turn up for practice at least fifteen minutes early. He stressed that merely being on time wasn't good enough: "If you are five minutes early, you are ten minutes late." That established the legend of Lombardi Time. It demanded self-discipline and an ordered mind. It rewarded proactivity and commitment. It is as authentic a concept now as when he introduced it at the Green Bay Packers in the sixties.

His sayings tend to be recited as if they are written on holy parchment. You see them in all their laminated glory in weight rooms and changing areas across professional sports. His insistence that "winning isn't everything; it's the only thing" has a bit of Liverpool legend Bill Shankly about it. For me, the greatest symbol of his legacy is a clock overlooking that often frigid Lambeau Field, the Packers' stadium. It was erected in 2012 and runs a quarter of an hour ahead of the actual time.

Call Out Inconsistencies in the System

Just as we live our organization's mission statement in reality, we must never be afraid to ask hard questions of those in authority. I called out Chelsea's hierarchy when I felt it wasn't living one of the core organizational values: that we are many teams but one club. That self-professed virtue was utterly meaningless because at the time members of the women's team were not allowed to use the swimming pool in the male section of the training ground.

We turned it into a bit of a joke within our dressing room, but I was deadly serious. I was determined to gain access to the pool and demanded professional respect. Had we let it ride, we would have been complicit in allowing the club to get away with not being true to its own values. Did we succeed? It took certain changes in the infrastructure, but hell yeah, we did.

Equality, inclusivity, and diversity are essential when your dressing room contains couples in personal relationships with one another, unmarried young women, wives and mothers, husbands and fathers. They come from different backgrounds and contrasting cultures, but are all invested in the same thing. Our success.

The team came up with the catchphrase "Is it helping us to win?" as a means of focusing on what is most important. It's a variation of "Will it make the boat go faster?" the motto coined by the British men's rowing eight, which was transformed from an underachieving unit to Olympic champions in the two years leading up to the Sydney Olympic Games in 2000.

In seeking to manage things better, we took the collective decision to break down issues into small subgroups. The process is transparent and consistent. Players are taken from different units within the team—defense, midfield, and attack—to work alongside a couple of coaches, a member of the ops team, and other support staff.

These subgroups convene within a day of the game and do not come out of the room until they have come up with a way forward. It avoids the blame game since the problem is dealt with openly. So, for example, if we arrived late at the stadium, players would have the opportunity to point out to the ops team that it compromised their ability to prepare optimally. They would be within their rights to ask for operational processes to be reviewed and if necessary amended.

That's far better than an alternative scenario in which players bicker among themselves and suggest they performed poorly because of circumstances beyond their control. The results from these reviews have become increasingly influential. People know they can be as direct as they like, provided criticism is appropriately expressed. That's led to another motto being adopted by the team: Champion-minded people always ask what can be better.

What is your process when troubles arise at work? Do you meet privately with other managers or share your concerns with a mentor? Approaching issues in a less hierarchical way by meeting with representatives at every level can lead to collective solutions and more robust systems.

It's a two-way process. While I was recuperating, I received a text from Jess Carter, a member of England's European Championship-winning squad. She had been substituted after sixty-five minutes, and wanted to ask Denise Reddy and Paul Green, who were running the group in my absence, what she could do to improve, and gain more playing time.

That took courage, to a degree, and the way her request was framed made a positive out of a negative. She was already in a better place than when she was stewing in the dugout, trying frantically to rationalize her disappointment. We try to teach our players to be coachable. We can tell them how to cope, and how they can develop, so they can be counted on. They've got to be competitive and consistent. It's our job to create a caring and supportive environment. The best coaches understand the person as well as the player.

At the end of the season, I meet with each player and ask them what type of person they wish to be remembered as. For most, being on the team is the most pressing need. It defines them, sustains them, and confirms their identity. Yet I don't believe you can't find joy in your work if you are not one of the front-runners, which in Chelsea's case would be a regular starter. Of course, you will have to be strong enough to deal with external criticism and the perception of underachievement, but you can still be a top professional, and a success on your own terms, if you are hyperfocused and aware of what drives you. Leaders should encourage people to become the best version of themselves, however they contribute to the organization.

Remember to

- live your team's mission statement.
- review the system first, the individual second.
- call out inconsistencies in the system.

Chapter 7

The Love You Take

Harry Richard Hayes came into the world on May 17, 2018. I remember it as if it were yesterday. How can I put into words how I felt, holding him for the first time? It is impossible, really, but I owe it to you to try.

Put simply, it was the biggest moment of my life. I was swamped by an emotional tsunami. I wept unashamedly. I was cradling this person I had never met but felt I had always known. For me, having a child triggered a love like no other and fulfilled a longing like no other. Nothing, but nothing, in the world prepares you for giving life.

The mechanics of delivery, whether the birth is natural or, as in Harry's case, through a scheduled C-section, are incidental. In an instant you are propelled out of your self-oriented, narrow, and predictable world into a new reality where you must nurture and care for the most precious thing you will ever know. Like every new parent, I asked myself, "How am I going to do this?"

The question had a poignant relevance. Little more than half an hour after I had given birth to Harry, who was whisked away to the intensive care unit, I had to deliver his stillborn twin, Albie, whom I had felt pass away in my womb several weeks earlier.

That remains the hardest thing I have ever done. Pray God, it always will be. It was an ordeal beyond comprehension.

In my more reflective moments, I understand the truth Carl Jung, the Swiss psychiatrist who founded analytical psychology, was attempting to express when he said, "The word 'happy' would lose its meaning if it were not balanced by sadness."

This was no time for quiet contemplation. The pain of loss was as intense as my earlier euphoria. It was a primal experience. Time heals, to a degree, but I still cry at unexpected moments and with the emergence of sudden memories. Anniversaries are still difficult to bear.

Motherhood has made me more aware of my vulnerabilities, but more grateful for life's blessings, more patient with its trials. I've become more accepting of my flaws. It has utterly changed me and made me a better coach and a more considerate leader. Since becoming a parent, I have learned the importance of appreciating what matters most to the people around me, personally and professionally.

Harry is my most important pupil, but also my most influential tutor. He is a beautiful boy, from the inside out. He is extremely sensitive and has uncanny emotional intelligence. I love football, Harry loves trains. I like going to get my nails done, he likes to line up cars. If I craved order and tidiness, he wouldn't have every square inch of floor space in the lounge covered with his train sets. He comes first.

I've got two sisters and I have always been in a relatively girly household. I loved my dad to the ends of the Earth, and the realization of his loss often brings me to tears, but he had to find his place in a matriarchal environment. Harry is a real shock for me. Completely different.

I don't really like half the things he likes doing, but if it matters most to him, that's all that matters to me. When I interact with him, I do it for him. I had some help trying to understand the best way to play with him, and how to be led by him. Being a mum is a massive wake-up call that has made me rethink my relationships with my players. Learning about my son has helped me to become better at managing people who are not like me.

Players come from different cultures and backgrounds. They have different value systems that I must maximize to help them fulfill their potential. Any role that involves responsibility for people has generational and philosophical challenges. How do you deal with individuals that you don't really understand? Where is that sweet spot, the area of convergence between the two of you?

I am a female football manager in a male-dominated profession. I can't ring up Sir Alex and ask how he deals with his players' periods, but I can make the most of the privilege of personal contact, learning from his authenticity as a leader of men. We do have a common interest as leaders in nurturing the next generation, but as a woman I have different challenges. That's why I have always supported players with children and young families. Their balancing act is delicate and difficult.

As I've already mentioned, becoming a parent will be life-changing for anyone, male or female. The difference between the sexes is one of responsibility. In most cases, as the parent who has given birth, a mother's care for a baby is more direct and, dare I say it, more profound. You nourish, cultivate, and cherish. You feed and fret. You nurture your child, physically and emotionally.

You have to do that as a mother, often while holding down a demanding job, not to mention doing the housework and the shopping and any other childcare. Mums from the sandwich generation are often also caring for an elderly parent as well as children, career, and home. Oh, my God. Juggling motherhood and my career was so tough for me, particularly in the early years.

When I went back to work after eight weeks of maternity leave I was breastfeeding every four hours. I would express the milk, put it in the fridge, and supply enough bottles until I got home. Breastfeeding can take a long time; hour-long sessions are not unusual. I found it a lot easier to express at 2:00 a.m., or when I began a new day at 6:00 a.m. The practicalities are diverting. I wish I had known of those portable electric devices that enable you to pump while you are driving or otherwise mobile. It's a faintly surreal area of existence, with hands-free pumping bras that are meant to be discreet and as silent as possible.

Dealing with breastfeeding, while being aware of your own welfare, in the midst of cleaning, changing, caring, and coping with chaotic sleeping patterns is hard enough without the prospect of returning quickly to a demanding job. You're basically doing it on the fly.

Football imposes its own reality. It is a 24/7 world. Can you really take a year off for maternity leave as a manager? It's difficult to contemplate, because your team is a product of your values, skills, and experience that cannot be placed into professional hibernation. It needs to perform consistently and continually. Could I have returned to the role after a year, as if nothing had happened? How could I have rationalized taking back the reins from good people placed in charge temporarily and achieving mightily? Should I have denied my team the time and commitment they deserve?

I beat myself up because work-life balance for a new mum in a highly demanding professional role is elusive. You have to work endlessly in my job or you won't succeed. Yet if I continue to perpetuate the behaviors of those in and around football, it means I won't change anything. Beyond the female perspective, fathers won't stay in the game because they don't see enough of their families and relationships with their children suffer.

We have to redress the balance. There should be a day nursery at every football club in the country. Clubs are bubbled environments, where there is an expectation that you've got to behave in such a way that doesn't allow you to embrace the other sides of yourself. That needs to change if our mental and emotional well-being is to be protected.

While those problems are magnified in football, they confront thousands of women in senior positions. They face a stark choice. Either step away from your career completely or take a very short amount of time off before learning to cope with a compromised situation.

I didn't expect my players to understand my dilemma. They're in their early to midtwenties. They're professional athletes, conditioned to thinking of themselves first and foremost. They want to play. They want to improve and achieve. They want to be given every opportunity for assistance.

Of course, they are going to be happy for me. They've invested in me and, hopefully, trust my guidance. They're going to be empathetic to an extent, but they don't have the life experience to truly understand the complexity of the issue.

We had only one mother in our dressing room at Chelsea, German midfield player Melanie Leupolz, who gave birth to her first child in October 2022. She is also studying for a master's degree in psychology, leadership, and management, and therefore has a broader perspective than most.

Players who have children during their career have, quite rightly, been given additional protection by a comprehensive Family Leave Policy, adopted as part of the reforms instigated by the Football Association and Professional Footballers' Association in early 2022. Under this policy players on maternity leave are entitled to fourteen weeks' full salary and bonuses before reverting to statutory rates. Previously they would be on systemic minimums, with enhancements being offered at a club's discretion.

I talk continually to my staff about normalizing the situation so that players will feel supported if they wish to have children during their careers. Of course, it is not as simple as that. There's nothing easy about balancing maternal instincts with professional ambitions.

One of the reasons why there aren't more female football managers is because it feels like a choice must be made between motherhood and the job. I should know. It's a tough position to be in. I wanted to do the right thing by Harry and the right thing by the team, but I had no real guide to follow or role model to ask. I've had to navigate the complexities of childcare and keep winning at the same time.

To be honest, I can't believe how successful we've been in the early years of my son's life. Having a child releases hormones that heighten your sense of awareness and understanding. It's almost like your own self-existence ends and a life devoted to others begins. It gave me a whole new perspective on compassion and identifying with others.

Before motherhood I was ferociously driven by the narrow aim of accumulating as many wins as possible. I was consumed by pushing boundaries, creating new standards. Those motivations persist, but they have been softened. I'm now far more invested in ensuring everyone around me is the best version of themselves while performing consistently.

Motherhood shifted my focus and field of vision. I began to see my players through the prism of being young people as well as elite athletes. They are not immune to the stresses of growing up, the struggle for self-realization. I might not understand them fully because of generational differences, but I am consciously working harder to improve my interactions with all of them, especially when these relationships are tricky.

It's the same in any workplace. There are people with whom you don't naturally connect. You've got to work at that and try to create an environment where people feel safe in their space to perform and to be their best but also to be comfortable with their vulnerabilities. I want to be totally clear that this isn't always about making everyone happy. There are differences and challenges like those that underpin every family. But motherhood brought home the importance of process: creating the right systems to help everyone in the organization thrive.

Here are three things to consider when returning to work after maternity leave:

- Negotiate new terms.
- Be prepared to redefine your own expectations.
- Prioritize family time.

My team communications specialist has a consistent message: a football manager is one of the only jobs where you're fired on a Friday and hired again on a Monday. So if you are a player seeking to thrive in that accelerated world, you will need complete clarity about the demands placed upon you. Training hard and preparing properly are a given. But how do you cope with not playing? How do you respond to managerial decisions you do not agree with, even if they are taken with the best interests of the group in mind?

As a manager how do you convince everyone to buy into that concept? Your most important message is that the team wins titles. An employee, whether she is a player, nurse, research scientist, or shelf-stacker, is a cog in the wheel.

A manager has to know who their people are. It's the sort of question that's rarely answered in perfect circumstances. I received my reassurance during my recovery period after surgery when I read a piece in the *Independent* by Magda Eriksson, our Swedish captain at Chelsea at the time. She praised my coaching staff, and reflected the caring nature of the culture we sought to create and sustain.

"A football manager is the public face of any club, Emma more than most given she is such a big presence at Chelsea", she wrote. "Even when she was pregnant and had her baby, she was so quick to come back; therefore, when we returned from the international break last week and she wasn't there, it really did hit you.

"Emma had told us that she would be having surgery and my first feeling was the human response – forget football, we just want her to be okay. Of course, we still feel Emma's presence. She is a winner through and through, though unlike some coaches who are focused on winning and might not care about their players, she has a really good balance – she is a winner but she wants it to be a family at Chelsea."

What a great girl. I'm rarely at a loss for words but found it difficult to express what she meant to me when she revealed that, together with her partner Pernille Harder, she would be moving on to a new club, Bayern Munich, in the summer of 2023. You don't really appreciate our culture until you are in it, and she embodies its strengths. Alongside Millie Bright and myself, she drove standards. Our experiences have been positive, worthwhile, and meaningful.

Mark my words, she will become an exceptional coach and manager. My aim was to create a culture in which players can talk about staff members in such terms and see the value in everyone. It is so satisfying to come across evidence that I've done my job on a human level.

A true leader takes pride in their dispensability. Magda's assessment proved I could step out of the environment I helped to create without worrying. It confirmed what we had built together over time. That it is not about me, it is about them. It's no accident.

While I was recuperating, my players looked after each other, pushed each other. Denise and Paul stepped up. The biggest compliment that can be paid to any leader is what your people do in your absence. The environment is self-sustaining. In Chelsea's case it highlights what we have built over a number of years.

Paul McCartney summed up my type of leadership in "The End," the last song all four Beatles recorded together. It was written in 1969, seven years before I was born, for the *Abbey Road* album and is only two minutes twenty seconds long. It features a rare drum solo by Ringo Starr and rotating guitar solos by the other three members of the band. Paul then followed far too many football managers and went all Shakespearean by delivering an evocative rhyming couplet. To paraphrase his famous words, the love you get is equal to the love you give.

Couldn't have put it better myself.

Chapter 8

Crisis Management

Thursday, March 10, 2022, was no ordinary day. I've seen a few things in my time, but nothing prepared me for the impact of a joint statement from the UK's Foreign Office and 10 Downing Street in the name of a so-called Oligarchs Task Force.

"Seven oligarchs targeted in £15 billion sanction hit," it read, in the sort of excitable tone the FBI used to announce the arrest of Al Capone. "Owner of Chelsea FC sees his assets frozen, a prohibition on transactions with UK individuals and businesses, a travel ban, and transport sanctions imposed."

Although the government issued a special license to ensure "football-related activities" could continue, the era of Roman Abramovich as owner of Chelsea was over. It was around 4:00 p.m. when I was alerted and started taking calls. My questions were those of any human being faced with sudden uncertainty: What does it all mean? What does the future look like?

The players' response, as they assembled for that night's game against West Ham, was uniform and understandably direct: "What the fuck is going on?" Their professionalism in winning 4–1 at the romantically named Chigwell Construction

Stadium in Dagenham summed up our shared values in pulling together during a crisis.

We were approaching the end game, following Roman Abramovich's earlier announcement on March 2 that he intended to sell Chelsea FC, with all net proceeds going to a charitable foundation for victims of the war in Ukraine.

I was given a relatively easy ride in an interview for Sky TV—whose crew, regulars on the women's football circuit, seemed as overwhelmed as everyone else by world events— before heading home to analyze the situation. The story led to news bulletins, and different strands began to emerge. I knew I had to take a step back and handle my own thought processes. A lot was riding on how I reacted. I realized I had to be calm and reflective rather than reactive.

Take Time to Formulate Your Response

As leaders, when we are in an uncomfortable situation our instinct is always to try to resolve the problem as quickly as possible. We want that feeling of discomfort to go away. But haste can result in knee-jerk reactions and poor choices. Resist quick decisions. Take time to analyze the situation and possible outcomes before you respond.

I was one of two spokespeople for the club, together with Thomas Tuchel, my opposite number in the men's team at the time. The tone and timing of what I had to say was crucial, both in public and in private. It was a complex, multi-faceted situation to manage. I had to get a team to perform in an atmosphere of massive uncertainty. By the time I was scheduled to appear at a press conference, ostensibly to preview that Sunday's home game against Aston Villa FC, the situation had evolved and the scope of my responsibility had expanded.

Sponsors had suspended support. A temporary freeze had been imposed on the club's bank account. The Premier League had disqualified Roman Abramovich as team director. Performance on the pitch was merely part of the equation. I had to address the ramifications of the sale of the club. I had to focus on reputation management. It felt as if I was defending my family. I had to be so aware of how easy it is to spread panic.

Spare me the well-intentioned lectures on the principles of crisis management, a glib term that suggests certainty and emotional stability rather than chaos and insecurity. You have no idea what it entails until you sense the apprehension and see the concern in the eyes of those closest to you. It is all very well to tell a small, highly committed group of athletes to keep things tight while things settle down. They have the same human need for comfort as anyone else. When they are unsettled it is my responsibility, as a leader, to reassure them by taking a carefully balanced approach.

I couldn't conceive of Chelsea entering administration but carried the memory of seeing a club fold. The lights were switched off at Chicago Red Stars soon after I was sacked in 2010. I remembered the stress, the fear that careers would be destroyed, and the terror of wages being unpaid. People froze.

With greater experience, accrued over the previous decade, I could compartmentalize the problem more effectively. I knew everyone was looking at me, waiting to see how I behaved. I made the point that nothing about our routine and the intensity of our work would change but promised up-front conversations about the sale of the club. I instituted a team briefing at 10:45 each morning to give an update on the situation, even on days when, to be honest, there was nothing to add; I'd be there, not just to impart bad or brilliant news. I stressed that my door was always open for anyone who felt the need for reassurance or more detailed information.

The mind runs amok when it doesn't have facts to digest. Sure, there were times when I felt bad or felt low. It would have been counterproductive to put on an act. I couldn't simply minimize or avoid uncomfortable truths. I had to be demonstrably human.

It was especially hard during the first week or so after the news broke, but I had to be really proactive. I was exchanging voice notes with the players, ensuring there was consistency and clarity in our communications from the top down.

I was being briefed by Bruce Buck, the club chairman, whose warmth, insight, and legal sharpness had made him a valued ally over the previous decade. As time went on, I was involved in confidential discussions with potential buyers about the scope and success of our program.

I'm a big believer in process when I find myself in a situation I cannot directly control or influence. All I can offer is my honesty and empathy. It is my job to keep everyone on the same page and watch for signs of people imploding mentally. The temptation for any leader is to offer an instant solution as a sign of their power and influence. Don't promise anything you can't deliver. It's better to be present, upbeat, and supportive while gathering the intelligence your organization needs. I was very conscious of my body language because when a group of individuals have their backs against the wall there are usually two outcomes: they either draw closer together or start to splinter.

My message to the squad was a product of the moment. "I know this is a shitty situation," I told them. "Stand tall. Don't be ashamed. This goes beyond an owner. You have a fan base, families, a badge to play for. We need to deliver for people other than ourselves. Carry that responsibility with pride."

I told my coaches they were second to none. Their work, in mentally preparing players for ninety odd minutes in which the only thing that mattered was the game, was outstanding. They reminded me of tutors at a military academy, expertly drilling recruits and readying them for that emotional moment they pulled the trigger for real the first time.

The media were all over us, but it was no one else's business. They might have wanted everything from us, but tough. They were getting nothing. I've developed self-protective strategies down the years and have become naturally resilient. There are steel shutters behind my smile.

Like many head coaches, I find press conferences a bit of a chore. I usually can pick up the narrative the press are chasing quickly, whether that involves social issues, sexuality, racism, or good old-fashioned windup merchants looking for throw-away lines they can twist into clickbait.

At that time, on occasion, press conferences felt like being the target during *Prime Minister's Questions*. Thank God I am a sociologist by nature and have an academic underpinning in international affairs. If you are tired, mentally asleep, or simply having a bad day at the office in that environment it can be career suicide.

I've always admired Sir Alex Ferguson's mastery of the press in such situations, and eventually I asked him who he was talking to from the platform of his press conferences. He told me his players were his only audience. To this day, I consciously follow his example.

I'm not ignorant or unfeeling and understand that everything changes when a war is declared, but privately I struggled to come to terms with the seeming inconsistencies in the decision to sanction. Who am I to judge, but hadn't the government spent years inviting wealthy Russians to invest in the UK? It is astonishing to consider what we have tolerated as a country and as an industry. The Premier League has never quite offered a convincing response to questions about other apparently state-sponsored organizations in the game.

It's legitimate to question the way Roman Abramovich acquired his wealth, but on a practical level—and even with the degree of separation he had from the club—he was an amazing owner who funded powerful charity work and passionately believed in the importance of women's sport.

Deep down, I knew Chelsea was protected by the global nature of its brand, and its appeal to a new breed of investors. It was a well-run club and would survive a change in senior management. I took nothing for granted, personally, but resolved to do as much as possible to ease the transition to new ownership.

I was impressed by the vision of Todd Boehly and his successful consortium. They knew from their experience in the US the social and commercial power of women's sport. Todd visited me at home for three hours on one game-free Saturday.

I spoke in his language, of my players' social media metrics. I pushed the marketability of our game and the authenticity of our philosophy. I concentrated on the opportunity of greater infrastructure investment. He left with four separate presentations on his laptop.

The deal was completed in late May 2022, and the momentum of potential progress has not stalled. I felt encouraged, valued, and above all relieved. Challenges awaited and change had been swift, but the perspective of considering new ideas from a different culture following a period of instability has been educational.

Football is still a flesh-and-blood game in which you are never too far from a crisis. It feels a little embarrassing to admit it, because there are immeasurably worse things going on in the world that deserve that description, but in our terms, on the women's side, that includes losing two games in a row.

That last happened in the space of five days in December 2021. The blue touch paper was set alight by the frustrations of a 1–0 defeat at Reading, where we were tactically dominant but would not have scored had we continued playing until the arrival of Halley's Comet. We had 77 percent possession. Our goalkeeper literally did not have a save to make after conceding a fourth-minute goal. We had thirty-four shots, but only three were on target. I substituted three squad players at halftime and didn't cover myself in glory.

One of the things I take most pride in is the positivity of our response to a setback. My group's first instinct is to insist "we've got this." They may disagree about the reasons for a defeat, but they commit to a full analysis, and agree on a plan to move forward.

On reflection, that observation sounds a little too happy-clappy, a bit too corporate. In the spirit of this book, here's what really happens. It's not the sort of stuff you read about in the media, mainly because it captures the nitty-gritty of performance.

Reassure and Regroup after an Outburst

I hate the sort of emotional outburst I made after the game at Reading. I was so angry with myself that night because I made some of my players feel small. I've trained myself to be better than that. I couldn't fucking believe we lost. I couldn't believe three players took something away from the team at halftime. It affected me.

All I did by bringing that up was make the players I brought on feel devalued. I can't give you a verbatim quote because I was off on one, but I said something like, "Why is it every time we rotate, we can't cope with the changes? We need to do better when we are rotating the team, we need the whole squad."

They all said we don't feel good enough. I heard from Magda Eriksson, my captain, that evening. Her immediate thought concerned the decisive Champions League tie we faced in Germany. The first message said, "There isn't a single doubt in my mind that we won't turn this around come Thursday. I know we will. But long term we need to find a way for players who are rotated into the team to be able to be the best version of themselves out there on the pitch."

She had struck the perfect chord. I texted her later that night: "I'm sorry for today. I'm sorry for my part. I'm annoyed. I let my frustrations get to me at the end. I will be addressing the elephant in the room tomorrow. I'll be focusing on what will get in the way of winning. We need to have a conversation."

I set the meeting for 10:00 a.m. and told my captain I intended to bring in Tim Browne, our communications coach, to help us shape solutions. Magda corrected me when I wrongly assumed the meeting would be between the three of us. She wanted to involve the whole squad.

It emerged that some of my younger players had really struggled with the way in which they were spoken to by one of my senior players. Dressing rooms are hierarchical places, so they didn't want to confront her directly. I called this player in for a one to one.

"Listen," I said. "I'm not here to discuss your football, which is great. But I need to tell you some members of the team won't tell you they are struggling with your tone. That's down to me."

Those sorts of conversations can go one of two ways. The player either leaves the room, goes downstairs to a mate and makes something up that frames it in the way they want it to be regarded, or they reflect on the conversation, own the problem, and ask how they can help. In this case, the latter occurred.

I had taken Magda into my confidence about my intentions. "She made it sound like you guys had a good chat," she reported later, then continued:

> I felt she took it in the right way. She respected your words and was mortified to hear how she had come across, and that other players had been feeling that way.
>
> The same thing happened to her as a young player, so she knows what that feels like. I tried to tell her about balance. If you say something negative, or point out areas in which someone can improve, you have also to mention the positives, so you get their buy in.
>
> I think that conversation did go well, although I did see some of the behaviour they mentioned in her game. It's just the body language. It's probably natural, but it doesn't look good. She took it in a good way and wants to know how we move forward.

Watch Out for Emotional Contagion

Emotional contagion—failing to recognize the impact of your actions on others—can be corrosive. We make assumptions about body language without asking what is really going on with the individual concerned.

These observations are not one-way affairs. I took on board a senior player's complaint about a particular teammate "being negative and deflated sometimes, which isn't helping." I understood her point because the girl she referred to was feeling miserable. Her confidence was zero. She was telling me she wanted to do everything for the team, but I didn't think she knew what that meant any more. She had lost herself a little bit.

The difficult thing about management is that people are fighting so many different personal battles. It only takes a couple of employees with their heads in the wrong place to destabilize things. It's exhausting.

This happens in every dressing room and in workplaces of all descriptions when things go wrong. It will not be solved by idle chatter. Work out a way to resolve the matter, or perhaps the player or employee in question might have to move on. I am a facilitator, but I have to watch out in case they start dragging others down into little silos.

The longer toxicity is allowed to linger unchallenged, the harder it is to remove. It's usually the end of a manager because it seeps from one to two to multiple people. As I've always said, get the elephant out of the room, whatever the elephant is. Don't ignore it. Bring it front and center.

In any case, at least Magda was happy. "I hope you felt it went well. Think the meeting was honest and concrete. Good place to work from now. Now it's all about shifting our mindset to the possibilities of the Wolfsburg game and not making the game bigger than it is, by creating any stress around it."

I thanked her, not knowing our troubles had just begun. The match in Germany the following Thursday was the single most challenging game I've coached in my career. We conceded four goals in the first hour and were eliminated from the Champions League group on goal difference. The result merely hinted at the extent of our problems.

Two days after the Reading team meeting, I walked into a training ground that had the feel of a casualty clearing station. Two players and one of my staff members had tested positive for COVID-19. In an instant we were transported back to the worst days of the pandemic.

In December 2021, around twenty of us had gone down with the virus. Some players were unable to travel home for Christmas. No matter what I tried, no matter what I said or did, I couldn't compete with the power of bad memories. People evaporated. They simply disappeared and sought their own space.

I understood why. Put yourself in Sam Kerr's position, for example. She hadn't seen her family in Australia for two years. Suddenly, everything was up in the air. She was desperate to visit her folks but knew as well as I did that the virus would spread in a team environment.

The match in Germany was a ghost game. We trained on the pitch without going near each other. Everyone sat two rows apart on the plane. People hid in hotel rooms. We went out, played the game, got home, and another four players tested positive.

Don't worry about finding the world's smallest violin to serenade me. I know COVID-19 hit everyone hard. I'm not making excuses or seeking sympathy. We weren't knocked out of the Champions League because of that defeat. We had been poor at home in other group games. But I was not in a good place.

As so often happens, I used Denise as my sounding board. Our conversation went something like this:

Me: We've had a disastrous week but fell so short it's tough to take.

Denise: Yeah, I know.

Me: I can't believe I didn't learn from other big games. We have too many that didn't want to do the hard work at key moments.

Denise: Agreed, or maybe they just couldn't do it.

Me: Either way, we're not getting it right. It feels like the opponent changes, and we are unaware or unprepared.

Denise begged to differ, but we were off and running. We looked at everything from the nature of our substitutions to the players' tactical appreciation of what to do when we needed a goal. I went through the process of how we arrived at decisions during the game and knew people didn't have enough clarity about their roles in relationship to the game plan.

We often do our best strategic and analytical work in hotels, sat down with a beer, so I checked into one in Birmingham and stayed up until midnight. I realized that I had to restructure the staffing.

I am pitchside, and the game is getting faster and faster. I'm relying on the information coming from the stands, the analytical staff, or General Manager Paul Green being fed to me in the right way. Yet when I looked around at the bench, they were all looking at bloody iPads.

I felt they were letting me make decisions without the full range of information that I needed to be delivered to me. It's OK to talk about generational habits, people with their noses stuck in a screen, but being distracted—even dominated—by the technology is unacceptable.

We then had five weeks without a game. We made the necessary tweaks and didn't lose the remaining thirteen Super League games that season. I was able to do my job better because those around me had greater clarity about what I needed from them.

I challenged the players by flagging the three trophies still up for grabs and put them into small groups to work out what would prevent us from winning them. Would it be our communication? The quality of our training? I tried to encourage debate and offered ready-made resolutions.

We reached a tipping point, stabilized, and then went on a great run. We might have lost to Manchester City in the League Cup final in March 2022, but we won the two competitions that mattered most to us, the FA Cup and WSL.

Sometimes you have to lose to take a step forward. Just make sure it doesn't happen too often.

When a crisis is looming,

- take time to formulate your response,
- reassure and regroup after an outburst, and
- watch out for emotional contagion.

Chapter 9

Coffee-Stained Wisdom

My journals, notebooks of all shapes and sizes, are scattered around my house and my office at the training ground. I have scores of them, time capsules that contain random thoughts, technical observations, and scavenged insights into the human condition. I'm not precious about them. Many are coffee-stained and decorated by the earnest scribbles of Harry.

They are as likely to include philosophical snippets and lists of books to read as hastily drawn session plans for impending matches. One journal large with a light green hardback cover, is the depository for issues, innovations, discussions, and strategies relating to my new adventure in the US. It is rarely out of reach.

I'm unashamedly old school. There is something soothing and strangely satisfying about getting it all down on the page by hand. I can use my iPad to draw up coaching plans, or download lectures and video clips to be used to set the tone of pregame discussions, but I love the way paper feels.

I'm at the time of life where it is natural to take stock. Sorry if this assertiveness offends (you'll get used to it), but I am at the top of my profession. My old team, our club, Chelsea FC, is up there with me. My new group, the US Women's National Team, is the focus of global attention.

Club and international football have similar priorities. What else can we focus on, and how do we plan to stay at the top of our game? How do we avoid slipping into the quicksand of comfort and complacency? Here are three simple rules, scrawled into one of those journals in the kitchen that I try to live by.

Rule 1: If You Don't Go after What You Want, You Won't Get It

So many of us are in a constant state of paralysis, thinking and talking about what we want to do. The goal is relatively easy to establish, whatever field you operate in. We might want to retain the league title. You might want to negotiate and secure a lucrative contract for your firm. You might be aiming for a promotion with another company. Perhaps you are a new mum trying to work out your next career move. What's stopping you?

How are you going to go after your goal? That's the question. There's nothing worse than empty promises to yourself, whether that relates to losing weight, earning more money, retraining for a different industry, or anything else dear to your heart. Just put one foot in front of the other and begin the journey.

The plan is a product of your behavior, a product of a process. Sure, certain circumstances can get in the way of that—social, financial, and education—so concentrate on the things that are within your control. If everything is equal and talent is the same, the top performers are those who apply every fiber of their being to the task in front of them.

Top performers are obsessive in their search for improvement. In football it goes beyond the tenets of training assiduously, eating the right things, and working hard. It's the details that are decisive. I challenge the people around me: what is stopping you from being better?

Say you are a defender who wants to improve your decision-making when bringing the ball out from the back. OK, how many times a week do you liaise with the analyst? What additional work are you doing before and after training sessions to make that skill automatic? The top ones carry it through.

One tweet, during the 2022 men's World Cup, summed it up. It came from Tottenham's groundsman immediately after England's elimination. He described the ritual of renewing the penalty spot on the first-team training pitch every day. Why? Because Harry Kane, England's record goal scorer, practiced so hard the turf needed constant fixing.

I found that immensely inspiring. That groundsman was proud of Harry. He took pride in his job, preparing the pitch to a level that matched the England captain's commitment. He knew the silliness of the loud, forceful voices on the radio complaining that someone at Harry's level should ping a penalty into the top corner without fail.

Harry Kane is one of the best penalty takers in the world, regardless of that fateful miss against France in Qatar. He rehearses and rehearses and rehearses. Circumstances were against him, taking a second penalty against Hugo Lloris, a long-term club mate. Harry knew that if he handed over the responsibility to someone else, and that person missed, the reaction would have been poisonous.

One of my friends, Alex Welsh, who was the goalkeeping coach in the academies at both Tottenham and Arsenal, worked with Harry when he was a goalkeeper as a young player. You'll hear a thousand youth coaches talking about what a player doesn't have, physically and technically, but they are missing the point. Harry is a classic example of the individual who refuses to let his talent limit his ambition. He has made the most of himself from the gifts he was born with combined with hard work. In that, he is a perfect role model.

Character is an underestimated asset, so take care in selecting the people you surround yourself with. I've turned down the chance to sign many talented players because, instinctively, I felt there was something that didn't align with what we were looking for. One of the telltale signs is a player choosing to bad-mouth someone while she is on the phone to me, discussing possibilities. I've had several reveal their true selves by putting down the coach they played for at the time.

That same coach had put them into the position to make a big move, by enabling them to grow and develop as a player. Speaking so poorly about someone so central to their progress tells me all I need to know. The red flags go up, and I won't let them anywhere near my dressing room.

Football is a brutal environment in which you are expected to demonstrate drive and ambition, but don't give me that guff about "this is the move I've wanted my whole life, and I'm ready to grind every day" if you are not prepared to acknowledge those who have helped you along the way.

That's why when I interview someone I ask them about the range of people who have influenced them. What did they pick up from them? What qualities did they particularly admire in them? What did they mean to them, as fellow human beings? What were the biggest lessons they imparted?

Maybe then we can talk about the candidate's level of ambition, their state of readiness to go all in. A word of warning to anyone who ends up facing me across the desk: I trust myself to sense the emptiness of those promises. Many are simply intimidated by the prospect of having so many quality players around them. It's tough.

My Chelsea players, you see, cherished the culture we created. They lived by an agreed set of standards. I constantly brought up our values. I referenced them, prefaced them, and celebrated them. I brought them to life. I shared my satisfaction when I saw us behaving in the manner we all signed up to follow.

It's all about the type of people you select to represent your organization. It's about stressing what matters when you are under pressure. It's easy to be a good teammate when you're winning. It's easy to be a good teammate when you are playing regularly. It's easy to be a good teammate when you've got a new contract.

What sort of colleague are you in a crisis?

Our collective approach at Chelsea occasionally led to some intriguing interactions. Rumors about potential transfers set the rhythm of professional football and should one of those land too close to home I might well have had one of my players knocking on my door telling me my fortune.

"Sorry, boss. You're not bringing her here. Don't do that. She won't fit into our culture."

I recognize it takes some guts to call out your boss in that way. To be honest, I love it. It means that our values are entrenched. One of my biggest eye openers was being sacked by Chicago Red Stars in 2010. Looking back, it was for the best. The club was chaotic. There was no feeling of security or stability. There was no foundation to help me feel supported.

As so often in the US, the players wielded a lot of power. They were used to expressing big opinions, even if they lacked authenticity or perspective. They could say what they want and change the coach's life in a split second. It was surreal because I was fired in Starbucks by Marcia McDermott, our general manager and someone who remains a close friend and quiet inspiration.

She texted me and asked to meet for coffee while I was getting dressed that morning. I was obviously distracted, since I then dropped my phone down the toilet. It was an old Black-Berry, and it didn't survive the immersion. Denise Reddy, my assistant, dropped me off for the meeting with Marcia.

She was obviously nervous but did the deed with as much professionalism as she could. I would go on gardening leave but couldn't tell anyone, especially Denise, until the details were ratified. That might have been understandable from a human resources point of view, but I still needed a lift home.

I "borrowed" Marcia's phone when she went to the restroom, called Denise, and told her what had happened. I made a point of stressing to her that if they offered her the head coach role in succession to me, she had my blessing to accept. I wandered down the road to Dunkin' Donuts and waited for her to pick me up.

Several hours passed. She turned up with her car full of her stuff. She had quit and cleared her desk. It was an act of profound loyalty that I have never forgotten. She had no severance pay, unlike me. She was an extremely talented coach who deserved the opportunity of promotion, but she made an extremely powerful decision—that she couldn't live with changed circumstances.

Good people. You know they make sense. As Italian football manager Antonio Conte said, "I'd much rather work with a good group of good people than great players who are shit people."

Leaders must learn how to read people well in order to recruit the right ones. Look for individuals whose values resonate with those of your organization. Ask potential new employees if they've had mentors.

Rule 2: If You Don't Ask, You Don't Get

We've just referred to paralysis. This second rule concerns passivity. If you are docile or unresponsive, who will fight in your corner? I tell my coaches and support staff, the team built around the team, that they are there to help in any way they can. That's what we do: we provide service to the players. Let's take the example of a player low on confidence. Until we know what she is struggling with—whether its defending, attacking, or transitioning in between—how can we help? Only then can we develop practical measures to rebuild her morale.

Sports psychologists might not like this, but that player doesn't need to be referred to them. I'm not saying there is no place for that type of support, but a goal scorer suddenly missing the target needs to reflect on the practicalities of the position. Is it a technical issue? Are you as inaccurate in training when the pressure is less evident? Are you getting into the right areas of the pitch? What has changed around you? Are defenses sitting deeper because you were so successful last season?

OK, so they are blocking the space you used to attack. Which areas do you now need to focus on? If you specialized in exploiting space at the front post, are you looking to concentrate on the back post? How else can you adapt? Are you receiving fewer crosses because of changes in the way our team transitions? Think. Is this a matter of execution? Is that execution faltering in a one-on-one situation? Is it a problem with a first-time finish? A header? Is it a mixture of everything? If so, what are you doing to counteract that? Oh, and by the way, what are you doing in terms of actively seeking support? Have you been retreating into yourself? Have you been paying too much attention to your press coverage?

This approach is what is known as the hypodermic syringe model, or the magic bullet theory. It is a sociological term that suggests messages are injected directly into the brains of a passive audience. It is the basis on which propaganda is supposed to work. The most famous example of its impact is generally accepted to be the mass panic sparked by the 1938 radio adaptation of H. G. Wells's *The War of the Worlds*. Presented in the form of a news bulletin, it caused thousands of American listeners to believe Earth was being invaded by Martians.

As a coach, I always refer back to the brain in crisis. How many times do you see a player dancing around carefree and cocksure when the team is up 2–0? The next week that same player, having a bad game in shitty weather, looks morose and clumsy, as if their legs have been drained.

Why are they in that place, and how can we help them? I remember the angst when Fernando Torres was struggling at Chelsea. He was missing his shots and couldn't buy a goal. People were saying that he looked short of confidence. What on Earth did that mean? He might not have been in a great state of mind, but the issue needed to be broken down into a football action. He wasn't executing because the communication channel between his brain and his leg muscles was overwhelmed.

His emotional core was congested. That meant he couldn't find the bottom corner of the net with customary speed and accuracy.

I'm fascinated when I watch a rerun of a match with a player on an individual basis. To give a recent example, I asked one player why she didn't take a shot when it was on. She replied it wasn't possible, because of her first touch. The ball felt too close to her feet.

You couldn't see that on the film. The camera angle suggested otherwise. It looked as if she was hesitant and overly cautious. From her perspective, it was much easier to square the ball to a nearby colleague. The light bulb went on. Instead of blathering on about her having a mental problem with taking chances, I could coach the technical execution of her first touch.

How long does it take to truly know someone in such an exposed environment? It depends on levels of maturity and differences in personality profiles. Some people prefer to handle their problems on their own. Others go even deeper into themselves and take more time to comprehend their dilemma. The key is that they eventually emerge and ask for help.

Ask. Accept. Analyze. I don't want anyone to turn up expecting me to affirm their status. I want them to tell me what they need. I will tell them to proactively seek it—not just from me or the coaches but also from their teammates. Be prepared for the truth. Otherwise, don't ask the question.

Leaders should make the distinction between asking a friend and asking a truth teller or mentor for advice. Don't ask your friend, because most friends won't tell you the whole truth. They merely want you to feel better. I understand if a player doesn't want to ask a natural rival in the same position, but pick someone in your chain on the pitch, like the defensive midfield player who shields you in the back four, or the winger who supplies your crosses.

I'll often organize "speed dating" sessions, in which two players go off on their own to seek answers from their complementary experiences. The questions are up to them. One that springs to mind is, "How can I be a top, top player?" You'll never know if you keep quiet.

Try some team exercises by pairing someone in your organization with another who is not a natural ally and ask them to offer feedback on each other's roles. How would they do things differently in the other's position?

Rule 3: If You Don't Step Forward, You'll Always Be in the Same Place

We've already looked at the dangers of paralysis and passivity. This rule amplifies the importance of proactivity. Change is a constant in all of our lives, and if you don't evolve, you're dead. To stay at the top, you cannot wait for the crisis. You must take steps to deal with it before it arises. You have to be extremely self-aware as an athlete, coach, or leader within top-performing environments to recognize the signs of decline. Champions are afraid of losing or faltering. They take action to prevent that from a position of strength instead of waiting to fail.

Likewise, when do I recruit the most aggressively? When we are on top. When do I adapt my training sessions most often? When we are playing well. What do I do when we are in a long winning run? I stimulate my players by overloading them, physically and mentally. Many people would do the opposite, easing off as a perceived reward, but I take pride in our relentlessness. For example, at the end of 2022, my response to a ten-match unbeaten run, which involved qualification for the latter stages of the Champions League, was to organize hard training ground games against male teams on successive days, just as the players were mentally winding down to their Christmas break.

There was method in what some will regard as my madness. The practice opposition were physically stronger, so my team had to cope with long periods out of possession. They had to suffer. I consciously cranked up the pressure on them at a time when I knew their brains were ready to enter sleep mode. I'd sensed complacency the previous week when we drew in Spain against Real Madrid. You can't afford that in any environment. Soldiers don't fight easy wars. They must be forever alert for the unexpected assault and guard against the fatal mistake.

Is your attention to detail greater when you know your life is at risk? Probably. But the point applies. Your work as a head coach, CEO, or the head contractor is to facilitate the application of the people around you. That entails bringing the right experts in, creating the right conversations, and setting the right example.

There must be a freshness to your work. The hardest thing about leadership from a position of consistent achievement is conquering that dread of "Oh, God, I've got to go again." The closest people to me, including former players such as Karen Carney, keep telling me they don't know how I re-create my intensity, day after day, month after month, season after season.

Victoria, my eldest sister, watched me at the FA Cup final in 2022 and said I looked bored. Well, I told her, I have won it a few times (five in the last nine years, if we are counting—and we are). "Why keep doing it then?" she asked. It was a really good question, one you constantly have to ask yourself, but the difference was in the experience.

The first time in 2015 I was caught up in the emotion of the occasion. We lost to Arsenal the following year; I'll leave it to you to imagine what I got out of that. The adrenaline rush gradually reduced over the course of our four other FA Cup wins in recent seasons. I compensated by making a conscious effort to watch everything and everyone. I made sure I understood the experience. This time I enjoyed it instead of being overwhelmed by it.

What Victoria identified as boredom was really absorption. I was determined to be as present in the moment as I could possibly be. There was a pang of nerves, a frisson of excitement, but I took it all in more naturally. I reminded myself of the privilege of my position. I may never manage at Wembley again. In my business, only a fool looks beyond tomorrow or the next game.

In a match in 2021, I was intrigued by my opposite number, Arsenal's head coach Jonas Eidevall. After what was a comfortable 3–0 win for us, the only thing I wanted to know was what he had been like in the dressing room. There are few secrets in football, and the feedback I received was that he had been frazzled. He had been in the job for only six months, so I could understand his desire to make a rapid impact. It was his first final, and, my word, I appreciate how overpowering that event can be. It is as if nothing else matters in the entire world.

Denise reminds me to behave like you've been here before. It might be an act to project composure during stressful moments, but it makes a big difference because you trust the instincts and rituals that sustain you on lesser occasions.

Something needs to come from within, whatever your walk of life is. I watched my carpenter build some cupboards under my stairs at home recently and was struck by the quiet pleasure he took in his work. He said to me, "Emma, I know you are going to shut the doors, so you won't be able to see what went into making them, but I know."

Pride in your work shows in the detail. Creating the detail is part of the challenge. It's the little things that count.

Enjoy your triumphs but always be planning for the future. That's the leader's job, to keep a keen eye on the big picture. Even when you're in the epicenter of success, remain ultra-observant.

- Avoid paralysis: If you don't go after what you want, you won't get it.
- Beat passivity: If you don't ask, you don't get.
- Be proactive: If you don't step forward, you'll always be in the same place.

Chapter 10

Voices

A thirteen-year-old surfer has her left arm bitten off just below the shoulder by a fourteen-foot tiger shark. Twenty-six days later she competes on a custom-made board, in the waves off the Hawaiian island of Kauai. Within two years, she wins her first national title as a professional.

A girl abandoned by her parents due to radiation-related birth defects following the Chernobyl nuclear disaster eventually has both legs amputated above the knee and surgery on her innermost fingers so they can act as thumbs. She later wins seventeen medals in four sports across five Paralympic Games.

An ultramarathon runner wins a one-hundred-mile race despite going temporarily blind over the last twelve miles. She suffers from hallucinations and falls asleep on her feet for twenty-one minutes during another 240-mile race. She subsequently sets a world record, running 283.3 miles in fifty-six hours, fifty-two minutes, and twenty-nine seconds.

More men have walked on the moon than women have competed in the Vendée Globe, a twenty-three-thousand-mile solo yacht race round the world. A forty-nine-year-old woman is only the eighth female finisher in history. She confronts fear and loneliness, lack of sleep, and handles the world's wildest seas while hauling sails well in excess of her bodyweight.

Most of us would be satisfied with being voted the greatest female athlete of all time. But winning six medals in four Olympic Games was merely the prelude to this five-time world champion inspiring a new generation through her philanthropic work in children's education, racial equality, and women's rights at the age of sixty.

Those women—Bethany Hamilton, Oksana Masters, Courtney Dauwalter, Pip Hare, and Jackie Joyner-Kersee—are just some of the voices you will hear in my dressing room. They each feature in videos no more than two minutes long designed to impart life lessons to my players.

Their stories are transcendent and personal but have a common theme of overcoming adversity, facing down fears, and responding to the challenge of being engaged in something bigger than themselves. In a world searching for meaning, they star in small but perfectly formed morality plays.

"I don't want easy. Just possible." This is Bethany Hamilton on her personal website, explaining her response to every surfer's nightmare. There's no bravado. She explains: "Courage doesn't mean you don't get afraid. Courage means you don't let fear stop you. My fear of losing surfing was greater than my fear of sharks."

She still sees beauty in the sleek killing machines, the monsters of Hollywood myth. She speaks of the meaning of being present, accepting her life for what it is, and making the most of it. She consciously cuts out what she calls "the constant barrage of distractions" and concentrates on the people and things that matter most to her.

Compassion gives her perspective. She could be speaking directly to my group when she says, "Courage, sacrifice, determination, commitment, toughness, heart, talent, guts. That's what little girls are made of. The heck with sugar and spice."

Celebrate your individualism. Leaders emerge from all sorts of challenging situations. Only you know how far you have come.

"It doesn't matter what type of body you have. Don't be afraid to look different and be different, your differences make you irreplaceable in this world. It is the determination to prove yourself that matters most." That's Oksana Masters speaking. She was born without weight-bearing shinbones in her calves. She had webbed fingers with no thumbs, and six toes on each foot. Rescued from a Ukrainian orphanage by an American speech therapy professor, she was adopted and thrived in the US.

Sport became her outlet when she lost her left leg at the age of nine and her right leg when she was fourteen. She won her first Paralympic medal in adaptive rowing in London in 2012 and won seven more as part of the US Nordic skiing team at the winter Paralympics in 2014 and 2018. She won two Paralympic titles as a cyclist in the summer games of 2020 and became biathlon champion in the six-kilometer event in the winter games of 2022. Oksana teaches us about the privilege and emotional release of competition, which she explains enabled her to express feelings that otherwise would have been internalized. She brings to mind a favorite quote of mine, from another pioneering Paralympian, Tanni Grey-Thompson: "No human being is limited."

Our own imaginations can limit us the most.

Human beings are a remarkable species. In 2020 Courtney Dauwalter received the George Mallory Award, named after the tragic Mt. Everest climber who died on his third attempt to reach the summit nearly a century earlier, for pushing the boundaries of physical human achievement.

She is an incredibly intuitive person, in tune with both her body and her brain. She felt OK, in herself, when she went progressively blind on that one-hundred-mile race. The course was steep, studded with boulders and sharp turns. She fell many times, injuring her face, knees, hands, and body, but persevered to finish through sheer mental strength. Her sight returned several hours later. Courtney is another individualist, defying fashion trends and conventional sporting logic by running in loose shirts and basketball-style baggy shorts. She tells herself jokes as she runs abnormally long distances because her reaction to them tells her whether her mind is in working order.

In an article on the Marathon Handbook website, she wrote: "I didn't realize that suffering is normal, or that our brains can help us overcome physical suffering. I was not prepared for the battle. Just like you train your body to be stronger, you can train your mind. It's amazing what our bodies can do but even more amazing what our brains can do."

Pip Hare, like Courtney, refused to acknowledge her limitations. She started solo sailing at age thirty-five and set herself a seemingly unattainable target of competing in the Vendée, the world's most arduous race in her chosen discipline. She had no money and little pedigree in a world where successful programs have eight-figure budgets.

She crowdfunded her entry and relied on the generosity of volunteers. She admits she was on the verge of bankruptcy when Leslie J. Stretch, CEO of the software company Medallia, stepped in to sponsor her just months before the race start. He was captivated by her resilience and resourcefulness and realized the power of her dream. She highlights the human spirit. It helped that she proved during the race that she is a natural communicator. She shared her experiences vividly, in a series of short video messages that captured emotions ranging from awe to trepidation to frustration.

One of my favorite clips captures her apprehension, uncertainty, and clarity of thought. She addresses the camera directly in a real-time dispatch from her boat distributed by the race organizers. "Right now, it is just starting to get dark," she explains.

> This is the only definition in the sky today. The daylight hours have been of uniform grey for the full eighteen hours of daytime.
>
> This heavy oppressive sky adds to the atmosphere of menace that has been hanging over this part of the Southern Ocean. It is a deeply unsettling place to be right now. There is not one sign of comfort or good times. Every feeling I have with every sense in my body tells me to be alert. This is not a place to relax.
>
> I know well that icy grip of fear and how it has the ability to paralyse you and to turn your brain in circles. But when you are alone on a boat in the middle of the ocean there is simply no one else to take charge. The fear cannot take control. It keeps you sharp, and you must learn to suppress it.

Suddenly, a key Champions League tie or a World Cup qualifier doesn't seem so daunting, does it? Pip is everywoman, the sort you could easily bump into at a bus stop. She is an ordinary person, capable of extraordinary achievement. She certainly doesn't see herself as special. She says, "I don't consider myself to be a particularly brave person. I don't think this is a characteristic you are born with. I think my sport has taught me how to control my fear and think clearly in a crisis.

"I do this not because I enjoy the stress or want to be a hero, but because I love my sport. I'm driven to compete at the highest level I can possibly achieve. With the euphoria of screaming through the world's most beautiful oceans on a beautiful race boat comes the exceptions. I have come to accept that at times I will be challenged, I will be scared but I will look the challenge straight in the face."

I relate so much to this, and to her. Veterans of the Southern Ocean (who incidentally include Mike, my collaborator on this book) speak of the spiritual nature of the experience. The sea has distinctive moods. It will punish or placate as it sees fit. It is not just a random collection of water molecules.

Navigating the great oceans of the world has a lasting impact on someone's mindset because the long-distance sailor is confronted by their ultimate insignificance. One rogue set of waves or a storm of unbridled ferocity at the bottom of the world, and the boat along with its crew can disappear without trace.

I want my players to identify with the open-ended nature of Pip's ambition. She could have retired with honor but intends to qualify for the Vendée again in 2024, when she will be fifty years old. She acknowledges that "my age is something that can't be avoided" but is committed to an athletic regimen that would be a stretch for women in their twenties.

Her fitness training, diet, and sleep patterns are all designed to develop greater resilience. Sustained strength and conditioning work builds the muscle required to safely manage the loads on the boat. As a full-time professional, she now has a team around her, yet she lives out of Airbnb apartments and travels relentlessly to fundraising presentations.

The best competitors are consumed by the next accomplishment. I can't be doing with this nonsense about you being only as good as your last game. No, you're not. You are only as good as your next one. Ask yourself: does my hunger have the necessary endurance?

This is not about sailing a boat. Placed into Pip's perspective, all these familiar slogans have a sudden relevance: Respect preparation. It doesn't guarantee a result, but it guarantees growth. Focus is a bridge between explanation, your ideas, and application, and how you will realize them. Threats are only threats if you are not prepared for them.

Visualize Your Legacy

Inspiration comes in many forms. Jackie Joyner-Kersee was a peerless athlete in the long jump and heptathlon, winning three gold, one silver, and two bronze medals in successive Olympic Games between 1984 and 1996. Her charitable foundation in St. Louis, Missouri, offers educational opportunities to children from low-income families, and she is a renowned health-care activist.

Her influence is seen in the shining eyes of one young boy in a clip that I love. He can be no more than eight years old, yet insists, with immense pride, "I want to be president of the

United States." This is about the perception of possibilities. You have to see it to be it.

Think about your legacy to others in your company, in your workplace, and in your family. You are writing it every day.

I often quote Albert Paine, an American author best known for his authorized biography of Mark Twain. "What we do for ourselves dies with us. What we do for others and the world remains and is immortal."

Ask Jackie how she wishes to be remembered—a question I regularly ask my girls—and the reply, taken from an interview from the website of Stony Brook University (located on Long Island, New York), is selfless, beautiful: "If people are able to tap into the essence of me, not just the materialistic side of winning medals and accolades, it would be as someone who gave of my time.

"Not just focusing on my athletic achievements, but on what Jackie Joyner-Kersee the person stands for and why I was motivated to do the things I felt necessary to help others believe in their own dreams. The most rewarding aspect of my work is seeing the success of others. It is about seeing them grow, from a doubter to a believer."

The athlete in her knows the struggle is as fulfilling as the success. It inspires a raw expression of personal faith. "No one can destroy my soul," she insists, in the Passing the Baton campaign. "To endure rejection, doors being closed. To endure people saying you can't do that. Know that you can. Always remain coachable, open. Be a great listener. Then go out and execute. If you fall short that doesn't mean you are a failure."

Successful leaders have failed many times over. What matters most is how you process failure. It should never affect your self-respect or your self-belief. One of the greatest challenges for a leader is not to believe that their mistakes define them. We all make tactical errors and misjudge situations, even as mature adults. Having the humility to accept we're not perfect and the courage to keep going is the hallmark of a true leader. Remember the legacy you are building. Where do you see yourself in five years? Ten years?

The team that had the greatest impact on my Chelsea players during these video sessions is the Seattle Storm, one of the most successful franchises in the Women's National Basketball Association (WNBA) in the US. Culturally, my players related to the concept of empowered female athletes, who use social media and modern marketing methods to push for social and political change.

They were listening when Breanna Stewart, who has been one of the Storm's most prominent players, said, "As women, we're always put in a position where we have to fight for something. This is nothing new to us. But to have the comfort where your teammates have your back, the franchise has your back, and opposing teams have your back, it goes a long way. There's strength in numbers."

Breanna left the Storm after seven seasons to join the New York Liberty in early 2023, and she will doubtless continue to translate the lessons of a great culture to her new team. Her peers understand her potency; she was named WNBA MVP for the second time in 2023, when she also proved to be an influential figure for Fenerbahçe SK in the European Super League.

The Storm players are so consistent in their behaviors. Their campaigns for social justice and voting rights through the Force4Change initiative are unique in being collective and organizational. Activism is nothing new in North American sport, but it has traditionally been expressed individually, by the likes of Muhammad Ali, Billie Jean King, Martina Navratilova, Colin Kaepernick, and LeBron James.

The Storm are currently concentrating on racial issues and supporting the LGBTQ+ community. They are reaching out to trans-identified youth, as well as focusing on housing, education, and health-care issues. The team uses basketball's urban popularity to explain why things are the way they are.

The humanity of their messaging seeps through. One film opens with Sue Bird—one of the icons of women's basketball who won four WNBA titles with the Storm before retiring in September 2022—going through drills in a silent, eerily dark gymnasium.

She is a familiar figure to my girls because she is engaged to recently retired US football captain Megan Rapinoe. At age forty-two and radiating accumulated wisdom, Bird's inner monologue in the video is poetic, and to the point: "If I could talk to my twenty-year-old self, I'd tell her people in your life will always matter more than points on the court. Every award is a team award, no matter whose name is on it. What may seem boring at twenty, like planning a future with the person you love, is the good stuff later in life."

Some of the voices we listen to don't need to be lyrical. The achievements they symbolize are sufficient, and their purity of personality shines through. Female jockeys have a higher win ratio than men, despite the perils of National Hunt horse racing, and Rachael Blackmore, the first female jockey to win the Grand National in 2021 and leading rider at the Cheltenham Festival, oozes authenticity.

Ireland is a relatively small, sports-mad nation that unashamedly worships its most successful athletes from all disciplines. That means Rachael is in constant demand, treated almost as public property. I shared her determination to remain true to herself by showing my group a short clip from an interview she had with ITV Racing.

"I can't believe I am Rachael Blackmore," she exclaims when reminded that her success is inspiring a new generation of girls to ride. "Genuinely. I still feel like that little kid. I can't believe it's me. I dunno. I hope it does help anyone who wants to be a jockey. . . . Keep your dreams big, I suppose. That's all the inspiration I have for you."

Take Time Out to Reflect

It's a bit of a cliché to suggest that pressure is a privilege, but what can my players learn from the aspiring chefs in a kitchen run by Gordon Ramsay? I'm fascinated by the stress of getting a meal out. You think football is hard? Go cook for fifteen hours a day with him shouting at you. Most stressful environments implode. People turn on one another or retreat within themselves. Why do they endure? How can they excel under such pressure? Are there ways to repurpose their techniques for our own situations?

I'm not naive. Professional sport, in all its forms, is ruthless. I make that point by recalling the quiet brutality of Magnus Carlsen, the Norwegian chess grandmaster who, at thirty-two years old, is a five-time world chess champion: "Some people think that if their opponent plays a beautiful game, it's okay to lose. I don't. You have to be merciless."

So, I hear you ask, does any of this contemplation work? Self-reflection feels like a rare commodity these days, a fact best expressed by Julie Foudy, who made 274 international appearances for the US and was a member of the 1999 World Cup–winning team that transformed the game of football in North America: "We had silence. We laid on our beds and thought about broken hearts, a friendship that didn't work, or what we wanted to do with our lives. We had the space between events; today's generation fill that gap with their phones, social media. Our biggest reflections would be meaningful."

It's important for all leaders to step out of their heads and their busy schedules on a regular basis. It can be beneficial to let your mind wander.

My players have little space to understand the meaning of life. They are hardwired to constantly chase dopamine hits. I'm dealing with a generation that doesn't know how to be still. It makes them anxious. I persevere because I know some of the advice I give them will come back to them in later life. The voices will still be there, as relevant as ever. They just have to be heard and heeded.

Think about the battles fought by those who paved the way in your industry—what can those voices from the past teach us?

To summarize,

- define your achievements by your challenges.
- visualize your legacy.
- take time out to reflect.

Chapter 11

Truth Tellers

As a leader, I have learned to gather special people around me. I know from experience that my job makes it very difficult to have a family life. I've had countless arguments with my sisters about what they thought were selfish decisions on my part.

There have been times when they didn't want me to work, especially in the latter stages of my pregnancy, and if I am honest, they had a point. But I am not a traditional character.

Identify Your Truth Tellers

Truth tellers are the people I go to when I need some straight talking. Like the mentors who had my back when I was growing up, they listen and clarify my thoughts by giving me feedback on my decisions. Look for those people in your network who you know will be honest with you. They are usually leaders in their own fields. Wisdom, acquired from contrasting cultures and environments, is invaluable.

Ausstrahlung is a distinctive German word that is difficult to translate into English. It loosely means charisma, or aura, although it describes a deeper, more subtle quality than that.

It refers to the energy an individual radiates, a source so powerful it has a profound influence on those around them. Sir Alex Ferguson barely coached at all, but influenced everyone through his radiance, his ausstrahlung.

That natural resource has to be maintained, balanced, and replenished for any leader to have longevity. Conductors of the great orchestras of the world must communicate nonverbally with their musicians, through the force of their personality, the depth of their knowledge, and the nuance of their interpretation. Ben Northey, chief conductor of the Christchurch Symphony Orchestra and the principal conductor in residence of the Melbourne Symphony Orchestra, believes this quality of ausstrahlung reveals the essence of leadership. The purer that energy, the greater impact it has on those we manage in our chosen fields. It brings together what he calls "the entire suite" of leadership qualities, encompassing inspiration, vision, decision-making, mentoring, and teaching skills.

Ben acts as mentor to the celebrated Australian Rugby League coach Trent Robinson of the Sydney Roosters. That's where I come in. Trent is one of my truth tellers, people with whom I share my deepest thoughts and biggest challenges.

Music has much more symmetry with sport than I once realized. One of my presentations to my players features Benjamin Zander, chief conductor of the Boston Philharmonic. On the first day of rehearsals, he tells his musicians, "By the way, everyone has an A. You've already passed the exam. Now let's get on and learn." Think about it. We are intimidated by the prospect of judgment from the time we start school, constantly worrying about what we will score in our exams instead of enjoying the process of learning and allowing our natural attributes to emerge.

It's the same with football. I almost want to say to the players before a game, "We've won. We've got three points. Now what does that look like? How do we get there?"

Trent and I always gravitate toward one another when we meet in peer groups organized by the Leaders Performance Institute. These are our safe spaces, where our guards are down and secrets are shared. You can be open and candid about your issues and take solutions from other sports.

The group includes pivotal figures from across the sporting spectrum, such as Gareth Southgate, Eddie Jones, Andrew Strauss, Dave Brailsford, and Arsène Wenger. It involves senior representatives from US franchises in the NBA, NFL, and Major League Baseball, and iconic institutions such as New Zealand's All Blacks. Respect is mutual and unspoken. There are sessions via videoconference every six weeks or so during the year, but our most valuable work is done over four days together in person, usually at Twickenham. Challenges unite coaches. We sit down, compare experiences from different environments, and problem solve.

To give a recent example, personally relevant given a shift in Chelsea's strategic direction under new ownership, we discussed the concept of global multiclub ownership models in football. How do you get the methodological approach right, so that standards and philosophies are consistent?

It encourages a new way of looking at things. The San Antonio Spurs, five-time NBA champions, gave an insight into the future when they outlined the development of their new training facility. It is regarded as an investment, with bars and conference rooms open to the public, who can pay to watch practices.

That made me reflect on where sport is these days. There are three facets to major modern sports clubs or franchises: the sporting element, the entertainment aspect, and the real estate potential. We are not yet at the stage where training grounds are open to the paying public in the UK, but I wouldn't be surprised if that is next.

There is a lot of discussion about managing technology. We've studied the value placed on instant in-competition analysis in various sports. How do we integrate our analytical and coaching teams to best effect? For all the technological innovations, everything comes back to the human connection and how we get the best out of our people. A whole industry has been built around marginal gains.

There's a lot of talk about artificial intelligence (AI) being utilized to help players to scan the pitch, for instance, but for me it has an element of gimmickry. I'm much more engaged by the challenge of constantly reinventing myself. There were so many similarities in the way Trent and I led our respective teams when I was at Chelsea. We had each been doing so for more than a decade, which is very rare in such a volatile profession.

I'm four months older than Trent, so we belong to the same generation. Ben Northey admires what he considers to be Trent's unique sense of creativity. Trent won the National Rugby League Grand Final in 2013, his first season with the Roosters, and became the first coach in sixteen years to oversee back-to-back Premiership wins in 2018 and 2019.

He is renowned for his man-management skills, which enable him to create contending teams under the salary cap by maximizing the talent of second- or third-string players who have experienced the least amount of playing time on the field. Those players speak of his integrity, loyalty, and humility. He has a history of brushes with authority, but although he is unafraid of expressing controversial opinions, he has a spiritual nature. We both believe in the beneficial qualities of meditation, both alone and group sessions at the club.

Great coaches create dynasties, both on and off the pitch. It is no coincidence that five prominent coaches currently operating in the National Rugby League worked as his assistant. They learned from his intelligence and his innate understanding of how to get the best out of self-obsessed athletes. Yet when we first met, he admitted to being a bit strung out, almost burned out. He had just signed a new contract taking him through to 2028, and he was wondering how he could continue to improve in such a familiar environment.

What did his leadership look like, having been with his group for a long time? I identified so strongly with that question. I was in the same headspace. So, three days before I went back to work after my hysterectomy, I asked my peer group, those truth tellers whose honesty I rely on, a series of pertinent questions.

Because my squad and staff adapted to a new reality while I was away recuperating, where do I exist now? During my absence people's roles have changed. They have a little more power and responsibility. I can't just go back in and put them back in their box, can I? What is the best thing I can do when I return?

Trent's response taught me the importance of a leader's presence. I had to utilize my strengths even though I might not be delivering sessions in the way I did before my surgery. He explained how the power and authenticity of your work can have as much impact as direct involvement. Trent helped me to realize that it is less what I do but more what I am. I can be a sounding board, a quiet reminder to staff as well as players that whatever you build over a long period of time doesn't always have to be delivered in the same way because our environment evolves all the time. There's no need for a unicorn because the success of the club depends on all the parts working together.

Any leader in this situation has to find another role, an adaptation of their authority. Relinquish control of the right things, because you can't keep doing the same things you always did. We both returned to our respective seasons, renewed.

Step Outside Your Comfort Zone

We take good advice wherever we can get it. Two senior US officers briefed the Leaders Performance Institute on the principles of the military and strategic operation that took down Osama Bin Laden. A UN peacekeeping envoy, a negotiation skills expert, was fabulous in outlining the qualities required to calm someone in a highly stressful situation.

I'll confess, at first I wanted to punch Andy Coulson's lights out when he walked into the room. The former *News of the World* editor, who was David Cameron's communications director in Downing Street before being jailed on phone-hacking charges, came to Chelsea to expand on his reinvention as a crisis consultant.

He spoke about the need to control, understand, and interact with a print media fragmented by the internet, and much to my surprise he changed my mind with his self-disgust at the damage he and his newspaper had done. His learning was enlightening, and his remorse was convincing. I wanted to pat him on the back, congratulate him on growing up, and for growing a pair while he was at it.

Other lessons are delivered closer to home. Arsène Wenger's take on youth development and contractual strategy was illuminating. But, above all, he demonstrated how important it is for an organization to be led by someone who is constantly educating upward, too, making sure directors and ownership understand the challenges on the ground. No wonder it was so difficult for Arsenal to emerge from his shadow.

Eddie Jones reinforced the significance of overloading the brain in the build-up to a game, specifically on match day minus one. His starting fifteen would play against a team with extra numbers, and he would manipulate events so that it was incredibly hard on them.

His example built on the work I had already done in that area with Dutch coach Raymond Verheijen, who is a force of nature, and one of my most valuable truth tellers. He is remorselessly demanding, dauntingly incisive, and dismissive of convention.

He is an acquired taste and radically splits opinion, yet I can only take someone at face value. I have found him to be an open learner, very giving to anyone serious about self-education. He is extremely generous in group situations and collaborative in developing new ways of working.

I have taken so much from his philosophical concepts, including the stimulation of situations that trigger overwhelming emotional responses. When the time is right, I consciously set out to provoke the team by being an outrageously poor referee during training games. I let challenges go, give imaginary fouls, and award free kicks and penalties on a whim. I will allow play to continue if the ball goes marginally off the pitch, provided it inconveniences my scheduled starters, the players who make up my best team. It drives them mad. They hate me for it, but it takes them out of themselves, teaches them self-control.

As you age sometimes you want less of the frivolous conversations that come with being around younger people all the time. I yearn for more of those deeper conversations on a range of issues. In the high pressure world I operate in, my truth tellers are more important than ever. Imagine how many interactions you have on a daily basis as a football manager. Everything comes through you. You are the center point of the organization. You walk into the building and it is relentless until you leave.

It's not just the player who says, "I know you have got a lot on but have you got a minute?" It's the staff member who says, "By the way, I just want to give you a heads up on this." Or the guy who says, "I've been working on this project. Can you look over it?"

You have the ops person asking whether you are happy with the proposed tour itinerary. Or a medic saying they're not sure whether a particular player should be on the pitch. You are consulted on budget issues. The equipment manager tells you about the player who puts a picture up on social media wearing the wrong boots. The communications person tells you what's out there on X (formerly Twitter), and what the media narrative is that particular day. An agent thinks nothing of calling you at midnight. Other staff members send text messages in the early hours (although I am also guilty of this).

Where is your own space? If I spend too much time managing my players, who then will manage my staff? It's a massive challenge for a head coach. The danger is jumping between the two responsibilities. You have to learn to recognize where there is a crisis point and react accordingly. This is where the ability to prioritize comes in.

Know when to ask for help, especially when innovating—your truth tellers don't have to be your friends as well, but they should offer feedback with total candor and professional integrity.

Do I ever suffer from self-doubt? Of course. One hundred percent. I beat myself up: Am I done? Why did I get that wrong? Why wasn't I quick enough to make that decision? What could I have done differently? What would I change?

It's cathartic, yet soul destroying. Your mind flies off in a million different directions. There are private days of self-doubt, worry, anxiety, guilt, and lack of faith and then, suddenly, everything seems possible. You simply come out of it. A truth teller will help to fast track that switch.

Don't Repeat the Same Mistakes

I have a hard rule: Do something wrong once, and it is a manageable mistake. Do something wrong twice, and it is a habit you must break. I'm not immune to the fault; I have repeated certain tactical formations and strategies against specific opponents even though they have failed the first time. I am absolute in my determination that there will never be a third time.

I've learned as a driver of a group of human beings that there are consequences to my fallibility. When I was head coach of the Chicago Red Stars, I was consumed by my limitations. I couldn't cope with failing to find the solution to a basic problem: the mistake of building the wrong type of team. I just couldn't face getting it wrong. In the end I prayed that I'd be sacked.

Creating a support circle provides a buffer in a demanding working environment. The recurring lesson of that experience in Chicago—that you must have the right people around you—is another reason why I lean heavily on my truth tellers, who also include legendary coaches of impact and integrity such as Vic Akers and Chris Ramsey. Getting their feedback is not meant to be a comfortable process, and I have become increasingly aware that I thrive on different approaches.

To rationalize my thoughts I need disagreement, which tends to be guaranteed by Denise Reddy, my longest-serving assistant coach. I swear, for three months after coming on to the Chelsea staff as an assistant coach, Tanya Oxtoby, who has gone on to manage Northern Ireland, was convinced that Denise and I fought every day. Some of the attitudes struck might be theatrically confrontational, and the language is occasionally less than polite, but we enjoy the to-and-fro because it works for us. Problems or issues are broken down, kicked around, and we agree on a way forward.

I sat with Paul Green, my general manager, every day. We are wired differently. I'll say I want to get to the moon. He'll tell me the rocket isn't built yet. This might sound strange, but my team is united by its differences.

My truth tellers come from a variety of cultures and backgrounds. I've known Debbie Ramm-Harpley since I was thirteen years old. She was my first PE teacher, a natural nurturer who recognized my love of theater and wrote me into one of her plays, *Veni, vidi, vici*. She worked in inner-city London for thirty years and has followed my career—but doesn't have a clue about football.

She understands creativity, play, and group dynamics really well, and now operates as a behavioral consultant and leadership coach, advising head teachers and senior executives. Her innovative approach keeps me fresh and dares me to be different. She often uses her perspective as a teacher and a keen poet to come up with creative tasks to challenge or reward the group.

I value people who understand me, warts and all. Marcia McDermott, my former general manager in the US, hired me and fired me. She knows my flaws but addresses them in the context of more than three decades as a coach and technical adviser, from the college system to the national team.

Her mentorship gives me clarity about what I am trying to achieve. She has a knack of getting to the heart of an issue and defining the help I need. She shapes and guides me so I can pour out my frustrations before reaching a decision. I'll let it all out, and then we'll find strategies to improve. She presents me with fundamental truths without making me feel defensive. I think of her as being someone who recognizes the needle that's stuck on the record because of some fluff. She simply lifts the arm, cleans it up, and places the needle on the next track.

One of the biggest challenges in leadership is getting your people to accept feedback. The aim is not merely for them to seek it from you, but to make it a regular part of their working lives so that they seamlessly accept and analyze it.

A staff review should be a dynamic demonstration of holding each other to account without causing offense. I pay particular attention to teaching people to be aware of the consequences of their actions. It is so easy to take pot shots at the colleagues you work with, while disregarding the potential impact on their self-esteem or the group's collective confidence.

How does your organization manage annual reviews? Do people see it as a box-ticking exercise where they are unable to share how they really feel or a genuinely empowering process where they are heard? Are there ways to improve the process beyond a one-to-one interview with line managers? Are employees encouraged to be truly open about their issues with management? How about killing the unicorn by suggesting that people come up with solutions to your problems? Surfer Bethany Hamilton advises us to "find your why."

I need to know if my players are driven by the people they work with, our performance on the field, or the processes we follow. At Chelsea, that was a three-stage process. The first involved the player defining which of our six core values meant the most to her in order of priority and the motivation they provided. The second stage used our values to review behavior and debate progress. The third involved setting objectives for the year, with the club and individual committing to agreed actions.

It is not a one-size-fits-all approach, but it is two-way. I don't believe in formal appraisals. The two-way approach is designed to stimulate great conversations. That work doesn't stand still; I'll do a couple of light-hearted exercises during the season so we can understand each other better.

My role as a coach is not simply to improve players. They are there to improve me, just as I help them to become better. They are my best teachers because they have the unrivaled perspective of being engaged in the action.

I watch the game horizontally, from the touchline. They watch it vertically, on the pitch. That gives them an insight into tactical systems, opposing personalities, and subtle opportunities. The most important thing I have learned over time as a leader is to listen, learn well, recognize the right moments to interject, and know when to sit back.

It's vital to have an external figure who advises you on dealing with dilemmas you can't necessarily solve with your staff because of their unconscious biases. Say, for instance, a player is dating someone else on the team. I need neutrality, someone who can counsel me on the awkward conversation that veers between the personal and the professional.

If your job is constantly putting out fires, it helps not to walk around with a flamethrower. Objectivity is critical because a dispassionate reference isn't contentious. To give you an example, here's my exchange with one of my leading players, who wanted to know why I had substituted her midway through the second half.

"Well, first of all, those types of decisions are why I am here," I told her, having prepared several clips to prove my points. "Looking at your running speeds, at no point do you go above 90 percent of your maximum. You either couldn't do it because you're knackered, or you didn't want to do it. Which one was it?"

"I wasn't aware of it."

I needed to get her to understand herself, so I showed her the statistically supported video evidence. The first clip reinforced my opening remarks, the second showed results over a longer distance, and the third showed her being overtaken by the referee.

"OK," she said. "I apologize for even coming in here."

People get offended a lot in that sort of situation. The complaints are usually predictable: she took me off . . . she didn't pick me . . . why don't I get the playing time she gives to others . . . why hasn't she spoken to me before. It's emotionally driven, and I know I work in a "what have you done for me lately" world.

My starting point, as a teacher, is to try to build an understanding that you don't always get what you want. We all have different roles to fulfill. That's hard for the modern athlete to come to terms with, but to be a great teammate you sometimes have to sacrifice yourself.

That's extremely difficult to get across. I have to be able to say, "Listen. I know you want to play, but that's not happening.

The most important thing is we win at the weekend. What can you give me, so we have the best chance of that happening? I'm not always going to give you the answer I want to give you."

If you want to understand what football takes from people, and how it can skew their lives, try to watch a documentary sequence involving Diego Simeone and his three sons, Giovanni, Gianluca, and Giuliano, who are all professional football players. They are sitting around a table, talking with brutal directness and honesty about him leaving their mum almost overnight to go to Europe, and having a second family. These are massive life issues, and you can see the boys struggling to contain their emotions.

Giovanni, his eldest son, tells him, "Football isn't your life. Family is your life. We are your life. You spend your days asking me how well I played, how many goals I scored. It doesn't matter. I don't care. I want you to ask how I am and what I want to do."

I cried my eyes out watching and listening to that. There but for the grace of God. Some truths are almost too hard to take.

There are no unicorns, just as there are no infallible leaders. Every effective leader needs a trusted support network of truth tellers to hone their ideas, so remember to

- identify your allies,
- step outside your comfort zone, and
- don't repeat the same mistakes.

Chapter 12

Run with Champions

We are the women who run with the best
That hunt and move and never rest
That play with passion and a heart that beats
With courage and tenacity. We're elite athletes

We are the team that makes decisions
In the field of play that ends in precision
That works every ball and makes the call
Which creates the chances for one and all

We are the players whose feet are swift and strong
That send the passes both short and long
That work for each other at every turn
When backing is needed, the respect we earn

We are the footballers that love to play
That train and gain skills every day
Who use our hands, and lend a hand
That punches the air and makes the command

We are the individuals whose confidence is assured
In times of pressure, support will be secured
That knows her resolve and never gives up
Whose determination is to win that Cup

We are the women who play with the best
Who have persevered and faced the test
Whose fate lies in the final game
And want the trophy with the Chelsea name

I'm no poet laureate, although I was proud to get an A in English at school. I gave a framed version of my poem, "Run with Champions," to each player and member of my support staff. I'm ashamed to say mine fell off the wall in the downstairs toilet and smashed, but I repaired it because it is as precious in the memories it stirs as my medal collection is.

As a leader it is part of my job to create hooks. I believe in marking achievement, so at Chelsea I organized a symbolic gift whenever we reached a Cup final. It became part of our culture, something we did on big occasions. These keepsakes are created in conjunction with one of my truth tellers, Debbie Ramm-Harpley. As I've mentioned, she was my first PE teacher who involved me in the theater productions she staged at school.

We are on the same creative wavelength. She appreciates what I am trying to achieve and helps me prepare for significant moments. I usually put a poem with a card on each player's chair on the day of the final. One year I gave them personalized photo albums. In the past, I've given them engraved gifts, meaningful crystals, and stones.

Occasionally, I give them seasonal flowers with explanations of their significance. A couple of years ago I gave the group posies of orange roses, to symbolize their enthusiasm, desire, and unlimited energy. This flower indicates pride and best wishes and is known as a traditional bridge between platonic love and friendship. My explanatory note ended with this message: *This denotes the inspiration in your life. It says I am so proud of you.*

I confess, I wasn't the first to recognize the potential of gladioli to make a point. Dame Edna Everage, played by the late, great Australian comedian Barry Humphries, used to throw her "gladdies" into the audience at the end of a show. Morrissey, lead singer of The Smiths, used a stalk as a mock microphone in protest of being expected to mime on *Top of the Pops* and, intriguingly, he felt the gladioli "seemed very powerful."

That's the sense I had, in handing bunches of purple gladioli to my group. Their long and pointed shape explains why they are named from the Latin *gladius*, meaning sword. In Rome, they were associated with gladiators, who wore gladiolus corms, or underground stems, around their necks during battles to protect them from death.

Gladioli were known as a harbinger of victory and associated with strength and integrity. For good measure, purple signifies grace. I know we are in the realms of performance art here, but at least they make my girls feel good. How do you nurture the people in your organization to show them your appreciation?

Little things assume exaggerated importance on the biggest stage. Maintaining an athlete's mental equilibrium is an important element of coaching. The psychology of performance is a subtle process, and I'm constantly looking for an edge.

I tell my players to look at what they have accomplished when they feel in danger of being overwhelmed by the occasion. Medals make you feel good about yourself, but motivation is an acutely personal phenomenon. For me, it is Harry, my boy. He's the most important thing in the world to me. Sure, the trophies are great, and they remind me of what we have achieved, but my mindset has changed fundamentally.

Earlier in my career, big wins left me empty, aspiring. The medals were nice, but it was always "What's next?" Now I am so happy Harry is there to share the experience. I can see his face in the crowd. My confidence comes and goes, but when I struggle, I center myself with the many good things in my life. Otherwise, I'd be fueled with self-doubt, anxiety, and a lack of courage.

Harry softens me. You can see it in my face when I'm posing with him, my team, and our trophies. I've got my bubba in my arms. All is well with the world. I don't ever want to talk about what I lost and didn't have in my life because of my job. That photograph is a powerful reminder of unspoken priorities.

I'm planning to give my girls cartoons and caricatures and will continue to use books to set the philosophical tone of our work. I give each player a copy of *Siddhartha*, the classic novel by the German writer Herman Hesse. I encourage them to find meaning in the story of a wealthy Indian Brahmin who rejects a life of privilege to seek spiritual fulfillment. He leaves home and finds inner peace and enlightenment in the many people he meets on that spiritual journey. It is about finding peace within yourself and understanding the importance of life's simple pleasures. It's a timeless message, applicable at any age.

Some players take it to heart. Most probably indulge me and think I'm off on one of my flights of fancy. The generation of athletes I deal with are consumed by everything but that simplicity. That's fine, a fact of everyday life. The book isn't a test they must pass. If it helps, great. If not, no worries.

Professional football players lead surprisingly restricted lives. They travel the world but tend to see little outside the traditional shuttle between airport, hotel, training complex, and stadium. Anything that tempts them out of that bubble helps me to understand them better.

Another book I constantly reference is *Man's Search for Meaning*, the deeply affecting Auschwitz memoir by Viktor E. Frankl, who was a leading Viennese psychiatrist before World War II. He observed that the prisoners who comforted others, to the point of giving away precious pieces of bread, survived the longest.

I paraphrase one of the book's most powerful quotes in my group presentations: "One thing you can't take away from me is how I choose to respond to what you do to me. The last of one's freedoms is to choose one's attitudes in any circumstances."

Frankl concluded that man's pursuit of purpose is paramount. I identify with the mental energy released by that statement, personally and professionally, but I know I need balance in my approach. I can't be serious all the time.

Sometimes, to lift the mood at Chelsea, we would borrow a karaoke classic. This version, inspired by "Go West" by the Pet Shop Boys, acted as theme tune for the League Cup final in 2021 when we beat Bristol City 6–0 in the final. I'll spare you my singing, but it went something like this:

(Together) We will make our way
(Together) We will win today
(Together) Our feet on the ball
(Together) We will all stand tall

(Together) We will soar so high
(Together) It's a goal we'll cry
(Together) We will push the offense
(Together) We are all immense

(Go West) We have learned our craft
(Go West) We practice hard and fast
(Go West) We will work and strive
(Go West) We've relentless drive

The rest of our pastiche of the song, which I reproduced against the background of a photograph of my team on their knees celebrating a goal in the rain at night, doesn't really scan musically, but it carried powerful personal reference points. It was a form of mutual recognition that feels intimate, special:

Harder flicks it in
England heads a win
Kerr cuts right through
Bright is up there too
Berger sends it long
The defense is strong
Spence is on the pounce
Erin claims the bounce

Ingle lets it fly
Ji dribbles by
Maren's on a penalty kick
Kirby's on a hat trick
Melly strikes it true
We cut the defense in two

There's a perfect cross
Magda is the boss

We know that there are many ways
To take our place for Emma Hayes
Together there is only one aim
To take control and rule the game
We must play our very best
To prove we can beat the rest
There is no compromise
We want to win every prize

There is a hidden poignancy to those lines. Football teams are finite things. Change is constant. Players come and go. Careers wax and wane. Several of those given name-checks in those verses—such as Magda, Pernille, Ji, and Beth—are no longer with the club. It's an unavoidable part of an athlete's life cycle.

Disrupt Your Routines

As a leader I have to be constantly on my guard. Work environments have to create discomfort, or the familiarity of routine may breed contempt. That's one of the hardest things to do because we humans like creature comforts. In my job, wisdom tends to be passed down by peers: I've had so many people with greater experience tell me to be worried if everything seems really agreeable and things are humming along nicely. You need a bit of tension. You need a bit of challenge. You need positive discomfort to get the best out of your players and staff.

What do I mean by that? It involves strategic disruption to the routine, a harmless electrical shock of uncertainty or unfamiliarity, usually applied when the squad reconvenes at the start of a new season. I deliberately change positions in the locker room so players find they are not sitting in the same seat. They resist it. You've interfered with the established order, separated them, if only temporarily, from their cozy friendship groups.

I watch closely to see the ones who cope and those who don't. Everything around them is changing. The last thing I do in preseason training is repeat what I did the previous year. The start time of training sessions, and their structure and content, is never the same.

If it ain't broke, smash it.

You have to draw the group back to a single message, and sometimes that is helped by not talking, because as a leader you have to recognize when you are bored of your own voice. If you are, they are. I'm not afraid to go a little left field to try to wake everyone up.

Sometimes I will put deliberate spelling mistakes in my PowerPoint presentations to see if anyone notices. I might throw in a math question or a sudoku puzzle for them to solve. There are certain routines you can't play around with in sport, especially in the hour before performance, but in general you can be as imaginative as you like to keep people on the edge of their seats.

I learned that hard lesson in my early days as a coach when I was frustrated because I didn't understand the potential scope of my teaching methods. Being different involves additional work, which puts some people off. But if it isn't broken, break it. Rip it up, go again.

I apply identical principles to my support staff. Whenever I sense someone has gone stale and isn't contributing effectively, I'll make a change. It might not necessarily involve a coach, although I understand why Sir Alex Ferguson regularly replaced his number two. It could be an analyst or a member of the performance team.

I'm always shocked by how many people come down from the stands to make sure they are in the celebratory photographs on Cup final day. I don't particularly mind if that is their motivator, and I'm sure it makes a nice addition to the résumé, but I know, deep down, some of them have reached their ceiling. They'll move on because I have to be continually convinced they are top class.

Change is inevitable, whether it involves, players, staff, or processes. It doesn't necessarily mean change has to be wholesale, because once a top-performing culture is established, everyone understands there will be moments when the rug will be pulled out from under someone's feet. I realize that might come across as being harsh, especially when I make such a point about the importance of empathy and basic kindness, but I have a job to do. That's always my starting point. I am paid to win games of football.

When considering your own team, do you believe the comfort zone is linked to optimum performance? Encourage people to come up with better systems, and reward those who innovate.

Trust Your Sixth Sense

How do I win? With a team. What does a winning team look like? What attributes does it have? I've been around long enough to know such things. One of the biggest skills you develop over time is that sixth sense for the player who is on the verge of decline.

That's when you have to balance your caring nature with a cold, professional ruthlessness. It is a difficult balance to strike, and many people don't want to have uncomfortable conversations. They prefer to avoid certainties. It's easier to give the benefit of a doubt, but I can't ignore it when my gut feeling matches statistics detailing a player's slightly reduced speed or power output.

That player will still be able to contribute, but not at accustomed levels. They're cresting the hill and about to descend. That's when I have to remove all emotion and distance myself from my feelings about them. Do I find it difficult? My God, these are people I want to be in my life, some of them for the rest of my life.

I love them as people. Some of them might have been with me for five, six, seven years. I know their families, their backstory, their fears, their dreams, and their driving forces. Is it difficult? Is it tough? Is it draining?

All of the above.

I have trained myself to shelve private sentiments, even if I can't believe that by deciding to allow a particular player to leave the club I am consciously jeopardizing or ending her career. Managing the exit process is the hardest thing to do in any profession, however many opportunities you have given someone before calling them in for the difficult conversation.

If the player is unhappy and doesn't want to be there, then it is easier: transfer her or drop her from an international squad and move on. The challenge at club level comes when the player's contract is running down and she wants to stay but you feel she has outlived her usefulness to the team and the group.

You have to be honest in that situation while remembering that old line about honesty without compassion being cruelty.

More to the point, you have to get the timing of that far-reaching conversation absolutely right. Tell someone of your intentions too early and they will down tools. That's part of the morbid fascination of football: you might not want someone because they are not reaching the right levels, but you still need them to perform for a certain period of time, until succession is assured.

Players will wonder what have you done for them lately. Head coaches are reliant on what players can do for them in the here and now. The reality is that it is not over until it is over. How many times have we seen players told they are no longer needed being reprieved through unseen circumstances and seizing that last chance to impress?

The supervision of the exit process is what agents and general managers are created for. It is the job of the head coach to keep the relationship with the player as tight as possible, for as long as possible, even if there is a mutual acknowledgment that a parting of the ways will happen. The only way that can occur is through consistent conversation. I have never understood football's horror stories of unwanted players being banished to train on their own. What sort of culture creates that unnecessary damage?

I hear it all the time from the men's game: "The manager didn't talk to me." Why? What's the point of treating a fellow human being in that manner? As a leader you have to be in the position to say, "Look, I know you're not happy. I know you want to move on, now it is all in the open, but can I count on you to deliver before you leave us?"

Male players are conditioned to resist emotional exposure. It's different in the women's game, even in the strangest, most sensitive situations, such as the controversy that surrounded Eni Aluko and her vindication in front of a parliamentary committee. The FA apologized to her and another of my Chelsea players, Drew Spence, following an investigation into racial remarks involving then England manager Mark Sampson, but the proceedings were uncomfortable for everyone at the club. My England internationals were being counseled by the FA about what they could and couldn't say, and it created division.

Some in the group at Chelsea regarded Eni as a friend and were supportive. Others were implicitly criticized by her for joining in supportive gestures toward the then-England coach Mark Sampson. I called everyone together, asked them to outline the issues, and determined we would not leave the room until the air had cleared. We needed to address such split loyalties openly, like consenting adults.

Everyone has moments in life when they walk on eggshells, but if issues are not confronted because it is easier to skirt around them, those eggshells become land mines.

Do you, as leader, want to become collateral damage? Trust me, it's avoidable.

To conclude,

- nurture your people.
- disrupt your routines.
- trust that sixth sense.

Chapter 13

Venus and Mars

Imagine the furor if six of the world's best male football players—Lionel Messi, Kylian Mbappé, Kevin De Bruyne, Erling Haaland, Robert Lewandowski, and Vinicius Junior—were to miss the World Cup finals after suffering identical anterior cruciate ligament (ACL) injuries. Imagine the money that would be thrown at the problem, the level of expertise enlisted in an accelerated research program. Imagine the pressure that would be exerted on the football authorities to protect their biggest stars by rationalizing the schedules to lessen the demands on the game's box office assets.

You don't need to imagine this: in the early months of 2023, six of the world's best female players—Alexia Putellas, Leah Williamson, Beth Mead, Catarina Macario, Vivianne Miedema, and Marie-Antoinette Katoto—were in long-term rehabilitation programs after rupturing their ACLs.

The new year brought no respite. Sam Kerr ruptured her ACL in the first week of January 2024, when we were on a warm weather training camp in Morocco. It was a horribly familiar sequence: she turned and shot, as she had done countless thousands of times in a totemic career, but her studs stuck in the turf as she twisted.

It took time to sink in, on one level, that she would never play for me again. We've experienced profound moments, which I keep telling myself can never be taken away. That's my default setting, rather than acknowledging they can never happen again. We have amazing memories of amazing achievements.

She was thirty years old and still attacking life, and her football, like a twenty-four-year-old. Her lifestyle befitted her status as a global star—she had spent the winter break shuttling between the UK, US, and Australia—but the game had taken a sudden, incredibly cruel toll.

Fate lies in wait. Barely believably, a little more than a month later Mia Fishel, the American forward I had signed to Chelsea as a potential attacking partner for Sam, tore the anterior ligament in her right knee while on international duty ahead of the inaugural CONCACAF W Gold Cup, in which the US beat Brazil 1–0 in the final.

I accept that in football injuries will occur and having injured players makes it harder to win. Being without Sam, in particular, presented a different challenge. On a professional level, every coach or leader wonders how they will cope without their most influential player or personality. But on a personal level, seeing someone you cherish and respect in such pain, and facing the purgatory of rehab, is crushing.

That's why it was such a joyous occasion when Catarina Macario, the US international forward I signed to Chelsea from Olympique Lyonnais in July 2023, scored within six minutes of coming on as substitute for her debut for the club, against Leicester City on Sunday, March 3, 2024.

She had arrived in the dressing room that afternoon with a cake, inscribed with the message "Thanks for putting up with me." Her social media post the morning after the game put the human aspects of her struggle to recover from her ACL injury into perfect context:

> After 21 months, 641 days, endless hours of rehabilitation, and many, many tears later, I'm so overwhelmed by emotions that last night still seems surreal. To say this journey has been the most challenging period of my life is an understatement. I went through so many setbacks, so many heartbreaks and doubts, that I thought at times I would never be able to play again. Last night made every struggle and hardship worthwhile. From the bottom of my heart, I want to thank Chelsea for never giving up on me, for supporting me in more ways than I can ever have imagined, and for giving me the opportunity to play the beautiful game again.

Suddenly dusty in here, isn't it? Everyone at the club, players and staff, was delighted for her. It was a reward for the unseen work done by our medical and performance teams, who guided her toward the light at the end of a long dark tunnel. Heaven knows, we need such feel-good stories.

To put the scale of the problem into starker perspective, between January 2022 and March 2023 nearly seventy elite players suffered torn ACLs. A quarter of the twenty nominees for the 2022 Ballon d'Or, one of world football's most cherished prizes for individual excellence, were recovering from serious knee injuries. From Remi Allen to Jessica Ziu, it was an A to Z of unnecessary agony.

Sure, there were calls for a more thorough investigation into the reason why female players are up to six times more likely to suffer a noncontact ACL injury than their male counterparts. Yet FIFA, unbidden, announced a new World Club Cup for women, adding to an already suicidal schedule. There was a renewed focus on the suitability and availability of footwear in the female game. Forget about men being from Mars and women from Venus. We inhabit different solar systems.

As a leader, you have a duty of care to your people. You use your platform to amplify fundamental issues, as I did in outlining the impossibility of increasing the physical demands on my players. You also exert your influence by championing the sort of background work that generates few headlines.

Doctors suggest only 6 percent of research studies undertaken in sport and exercise science relate exclusively to women. That's why one of the things of which I am most proud is the lead taken by Chelsea FC in monitoring our players and examining the links between the menstrual cycle, hormonal changes, and injury. It is a very complex subject, which I will attempt to simplify. It might not seem applicable outside the sporting environment, but these observations form part of the female experience.

First, this isn't about luck. Mark Stinson, an American man who has been hit four times by lightning, is unlucky. He suffers from severe headaches and short-term memory loss and likens the experience to being covered with ants and scalding water. On the other hand, a player who suffers serious injury because of gaps in our knowledge into how the menstrual cycle can affect the physiology and biomechanics of the female body is a victim of the system.

In coaching, we utilize what we call periodization. Russian physiologist Leo Matveyev initially developed this in 1964 and it has evolved under innovative modern coaches such as Raymond Verheijen. Periodization is a structured framework for fitness with gradual progressions in things such as training loads. Every individual has different needs, but the aim is to reduce risk by avoiding huge spikes in exertion and the accumulation of stressors that can cause injuries. This framework is aligned to football-based principles, and a phase-based approach to rehabilitation and to the preventive programs we refer to as "prehab." It is also dictated by special consideration of women's health, nutrition, and movement. I don't believe that the men's game obsesses about players having enough omega-3 or vitamin D. We do. In the women's game, our issue, in general terms, is that we have insufficient scientific knowledge and expertise.

So many different elements go into training a female player. Are injuries caused due to anatomical differences? Might genetics play a part? Do we need to pay greater attention to how our bodies are fueled? How does all this play into an understanding of the menstrual cycle?

Before Sam was struck down, we had not suffered an ACL injury at Chelsea since Deanna Cooper, a defender who subsequently joined Reading, was hurt in 2017. We based all our movement and strength work on where each individual is in their cycle. To give a specific instance, our prehab program was designed around how to "wake up" the knee in a certain way so that it is prepared for the impact training and competition in the especially sensitive fourth phase of a player's period. In general, women should menstruate between day 23 and 28 of their cycle, which we break up into four phases. The first, between day 1 and day 5 or 6, is when a woman moves into what we call a high hormone phase. Estrogen, a natural energy-giving lubricant, is rising. So is progesterone, which helps us sleep and protects the uterus.

The levels of these hormones decline during ovulation in phase 2, which occurs around day 12. This is when a woman is most fertile, but that drop in estrogen and progesterone makes a woman more vulnerable to injury. This drop can impact upon the collagen in the joints, which become looser and unstable. There's also a neural response, leading to a greater sense of vulnerability and sensitivity.

Since we monitor our players' cycles very closely, we start to see patterns. A certain player might feel a muscle injury such as a tight hamstring during ovulation. Another player might suffer delayed onset muscle soreness and become what we call a little "DOMSy" during phase three of the cycle, which is quite a low hormone period.

We shouldn't fear just ACL injuries. We should talk about all of the possible injuries in their entirety. Women don't suffer groin strains with the same propensity as men, but we do suffer pain in that area, usually from muscular overuse and, in some serious cases, because of cysts. But our greater susceptibility to hamstring problems can be dictated by pelvic inflammation. We have had no option but to learn to manage a player's welfare differently.

To give another example, relaxin is a hormone produced by the ovaries and placenta. It is important in preparation for childbirth because it relaxes the ligaments in the pelvis and softens and widens the cervix. It allows our hips to tilt and stretch. That's why, in phase four, just before we menstruate, our joint laxity is at its greatest. So, on a basic coaching level, is stretching a good idea? Manual dexterity declines, so reaction times decrease. I'd be curious to know how many female goalkeepers who make handling errors on seemingly straightforward shots are going through that period of their cycle.

What can we do to wake a player's brain up? At Chelsea we introduced daily brain activation exercises, supervised in the warm-up by our goalkeeping coach. It's noncontextual, in that it is not about a football movement, but if it helps to improve reaction times in phase four, it's done its job.

Likewise, if we had a player with a substantial injury history in the fourth phase of her cycle—for example, Maren Mjelde, Norway's captain—we reduced her loading. We might have her do only half of a high intensity 4-on-4 session, where the continual turns add to the stress on the body.

Everything is individualized. Fran Kirby has a long-term issue with immunity, and with the additional complication of postmatch travel, we would pay special attention to her training capacity in the three days after a game. There are differences in approach between players who are on contraception and those who are not.

Training methodology rarely enters the wider discussion involving ACL injuries, but it can offer clues that are easy to miss. Someone like Beth Mead had been playing virtually nonstop because of her importance to club and country. I am not casting aspersions on anyone who worked with her for Arsenal and England, because both are elite environments, but had she been my player I would have monitored her high-speed runs, accelerations, and decelerations, and studied her RPE (rate of perceived exertion) for each session and game.

I would have been on the lookout for other potential indicators of fatigue, such as a drop-off in specific football actions in training. Rest and recovery are paramount, but this whole area is deceptively complex. Anyone can monitor a player's cycle, but what are we doing with the information to tie everything together? It's not straightforward. There is a huge disparity in professional expertise across our game.

I am a big believer in the innovative work of Stacy Sims, a globally recognized exercise physiologist and nutrition scientist from the US who points out the absurdity of the assumption that women are just smaller versions of men when it comes to exercise, nutrition, and medicine.

It takes a man six months on average to come back from a torn ACL, as opposed to nine months for a woman. In simple terms, we don't have the same muscle definition because we don't produce as much testosterone.

As a middle-aged woman with low levels of testosterone, I'd recommend strength training to anyone of my generation. Weight lifting can increase your bone density and testosterone production, and it may prevent you from getting osteoporosis in later life.

If I was a player recovering from a long-term injury and my support team trained me in exactly the same way that they would train my male equivalent, I would be in big trouble. I need to be in the gym building muscular strength, not working on the grass, which is the usual approach in the men's game.

I seek to learn from others' failures. One of the biggest women's clubs in continental Europe recently suffered a rash of ACL injuries. The number of these cases seemed extreme. I realized why when I monitored the intensity of their training programs. Taking into account the risk factors we have discussed here, the lack of freshness is potentially calamitous. No wonder these players were vulnerable.

Women's football is evolving rapidly, but the infrastructure still hasn't caught up. There are a lot of newbies coming in and learning on the job. That leads to horror stories of inexperienced sports scientists lecturing players about their body mass index (BMI) without understanding that fat levels fluctuate during the menstrual cycle. Imagine the damage that can cause to a young athlete's psyche. Some players are already prone to eating disorders, which result in undernourishment and elongated irregular periods, and carry the threat of constant stress fractures.

Where, for instance, is the expertise in dealing with the player who comes back from giving birth and who is massively underweight? I understand all too well the difficulties of motherhood, of being unable to find the time to eat due to the demands of a new baby. A player in this case will have relative energy deficiency. Before being reintroduced to training on the grass, her nutritional program must be prioritized. Until that is corrected it would be wrong to expose her to a high-impact situation. Her bones are simply too fragile. They will break.

It is our duty as coaches and leaders to be educated on this sort of stuff, yet the system is letting everyone down. Throughout my career development, from UEFA B license to A, and on to my UEFA Pro License with the FA, none of the modules were specifically developed around the women's game. I've had to be self-sufficient in my learning. Experience—gained through Sam Kerr's international commitments for Australia— has taught me that it is absolutely critical when possible not to overload a player for seventy-two hours after a long-haul flight. Ignoring that will invite damaging levels of inflammation. That's another cause of ACL injuries, in addition to fatigue, vagaries of the period, genetics, and training load.

What could happen? You guessed it. If Sam flies to Australia from Heathrow on a Sunday morning, disembarking on Monday evening, Sydney time, she might do a light recovery session on the Tuesday. She really shouldn't be doing what I refer to as intensive actions for a minimum of forty-eight hours, yet she will be playing in an international match on the Wednesday. These situations are simply not discussed in a wider context.

The most alarming thing is the lack of research. I will continue to call out the lack of support from the football authorities, because they are failing in their moral duty. They have the resources to devote time and money to increasing understanding of the problem, but not, it seems, the sufficient will to do so.

Chelsea will, I'm sure, continue to take the initiative long after I'm gone. There is an obvious competitive advantage from keeping your best players on the pitch, but there is also an acute sense of responsibility for the welfare of vulnerable young women in your squad.

I make a point of hiring open-minded people for my sports science team. They need to be good researchers because without broader systemic support in-house expertise is vital. We do a huge amount of work on individualization internally simply because there is limited external investigation in that area.

I hear so many people say, "Oh these things happen, you've just got to accept them." They trot out the old line that we play too many games, which is misleading, in isolation from other health issues. Some even blame the V-shaped female anatomic frame. It's bullshit. Injuries are largely caused by ignorance and a lack of education.

The levels of expedience are disturbing. I hear of coaches around the world giving female athletes an IUD to keep them in an optimal high hormone state. I've heard of others putting players on the contraceptive pill. Think about that for a minute. It should be the player's choice, as a woman, to make such an intimate decision. It is obscene to be pressured into it so something as ultimately superficial as sporting success can be pursued with greater confidence and effectiveness.

Little wonder scores of girls are leaving sport at young ages, not just at the elite end. A UK study in August 2023 found that girls are three times more likely to leave football by their late teens than boys. Body image was cited as one of the principal factors. I have had fascinating and challenging conversations with the research team at Nike about why they do not drill down deeper into the reasons for the dropout rate. It would make good business sense for them to counter them, yet it has taken years for the simple step of giving players an alternative to white shorts to guard against the embarrassment of natural seepages during a period.

How sad is it that we are only just at that stage? This isn't about white shorts, per se, but about at what point our industry—and by extension the wider world—gets real.

To avoid any doubts, I was born with wide hips and boobs for a reason: to give birth, and to give my baby milk. Oh, and by the way, boys, your brain is wired differently than mine. Why then are we conditioned to blur the boundaries in sport?

There are books written about the alpha male mindset. There is very little mention of the alpha female. The characteristics are not that different: we probably have a little less bravado, a bit more natural vulnerability. In terms of personality profiles, using the Hartman Color Code assessment, alpha females are reds. In my case, it confirms I'm comfortable with wielding authority. I am task-driven, determined, and logical. I'm proactive, pragmatic, independent, farsighted, and decisive.

What of the rest? If reds are regarded as power wielders, blues tend to be driven by selflessness, intimacy, and a sense of purpose. They value personal relationships and can be relied on to be loyal, sincere, and thoughtful. Whites are renowned as peacekeepers, known for their clarity, kindness, adaptability, and patience. Yellows just wanna have fun. They live for the moment and exude enthusiasm, optimism, and sociability. Well, that's what the computer says, anyway.

The leaders in my team mirror those characteristics, but I have to temper some of their alpha female traits. I may share some of their frustrations—"I don't care if she is pissed off, she has to understand we are trying to win the biggest prizes"—but I also know you cannot leave anyone behind in a female dressing room. The sense of isolation can be overwhelming.

One of my biggest challenges was persuading my starting eleven that they needed to show a better appreciation of those who were not playing. Their struggle to do so, due to the pressure exerted by expectations of continued success, signaled to me that we are moving toward a situation where we appear to care less about those around us.

That's where men and women's football may be starting to merge. There is no consideration of deeper feelings in a male dressing room. I've had deep conversations with many ex-pros, some of whom were household names at Chelsea, and they admitted to struggling to cope in such an alpha environment. As loyal husbands they were uncomfortable with attitudes toward women, yet they were conditioned to accept the culture of braying and bullying. They hated playing along with the party boys, so-called good lads fueled by bravado, testosterone, and fame.

Women players may be sarcastic and become disruptive in a subversive way, but they are not as antisocial as their male counterparts. Women players won't explode with their frustrations and let it go. In a way, that's a shame, because then issues fester.

I'm used to firefighting. I'll call people out. It's a case of saying, "Come here you. Got a problem? What's the matter? What's the issue?" They'll usually reply, "Oh, nothing." That gets me going: "Well, then, why are you running around looking all moody? Talk about it. Be an adult about it."

You have to give people your time. A simple conversation doesn't last five minutes. It goes on for forty-five minutes, and you may have three of those in a single day, some of them long after we've left the training ground. Glenys, my nanny and all-around guardian angel, says she doesn't know how I do it.

To be candid, it's a lot easier to do your job, on so many levels, when you get past that point of caring. If you start thinking *Oh my god, she's offended, she's upset,* you'll be thinking emotionally, and you won't be able to make the most critical decisions.

It doesn't mean you've got to walk over people, either. As a leader, you've got to stick to task, stay on track, and not get sucked in by extraneous issues. For me, the greatest strength in people at the top in their respective field is to eliminate the noise.

It's not straightforward, because it concerns how you say things, not just what you say. As I've mentioned before, the tone and timing of interactions are critical. Lose someone through momentary lack of thought, and it is a long way back.

Let's face it, women are often more complex characters. They'll hold onto things, remind you of them, and gossip about them. It will leave some of my male staff, bless them, tearing their hair out. They simply don't understand what's going on.

I'm proud of the initiative our medical team at Chelsea took to bring Emma Brockwell on board as our pelvic-floor coach. Her expertise is crucial for all women, regardless of whether they have had children. Emma has been invaluable in helping our German midfield player Melanie Leupolz come back from her pregnancy, and she has been a catalyst for an important debate on how women are treated in the working world.

I did a TV interview on the subject and was struck by a message I later received from Michelle Baynham, founder of the platform Mother Fit. She said, "The lack of support for female employees who either become pregnant or have recently given birth is unacceptable.

"I know first-hand how challenging it can be, working whilst pregnant, taking maternity leave and returning to work as a different person. Lots of employers offer well-being packages for the 'general population' which is not specific or safe enough for what could be the most challenging time of a woman's life."

I've always thought, hands down, it would be so much easier to coach in the men's game.

So, to summarize,

- don't expect one homogenous approach to work for everyone.
- recognize the specific health-care needs of women.
- listen to the women on your teams and create a culture that supports them in the ways that matter.

Chapter 14

Suffragette City

There's a photograph in its original walnut frame on my kitchen wall. A Christmas present from my Auntie Pat, it depicts the arrest of suffragette leader Emmeline Pankhurst in London's Victoria Street on February 13, 1908. It was taken by my great-uncle, my grandmother's brother.

My God, what a woman. Her head is thrown back in defiance. She radiates courage and dignity. Her disdain for the sergeant, grasping her left wrist, is heroic. Six more mustachioed policemen mill around, staring uncomfortably at the camera and trying hard to look important.

The following day, Pankhurst was jailed for six weeks, having been found guilty of obstructing an officer while on a deputation to the House of Commons. She was apparently limping, having been injured in a scuffle with Liberal Party supporters at a by-election in Devon a couple of weeks earlier.

She believed in "deeds, not words." I so relate to another of her most famous sayings: "Once they are aroused, once they are determined, nothing on Earth and nothing in heaven will make women give way; it is impossible."

You tell 'em, girl.

Pave the Way for the Next Generation

Like most people who find themselves in a prominent social position because of their job, I feel a responsibility to be front and center in an important debate. I didn't ask to be a reference point for people, but I'm happy to influence in whatever way I can.

When they tell me I am inspirational I wonder what that actually means. Is it just because I'm there? My visibility, as a successful woman, is in itself the inspiration. It goes beyond football, although both male and female coaches reach out to me for advice about their career choices.

The other day I was approached via email (as so often happens) by a senior female executive in the airline industry who wanted to share managerial processes and philosophies. There's someone who needs an impressive grasp of detail, and who has to be ready to take rapid, far-reaching decisions. Look around. It is not hard to find evidence of how sport lags behind the rest of the working world. Its prevailing culture limits opportunity.

Are barricades erected on Harley Street to keep out leading female neurologists or the best female chiropractors? Of course not. They are judged on their own terms, on their own talents. Some of the crustier, dustier elements of the medical establishment might not be thrilled, but equality is seen to work.

Hierarchically, female managers and coaches have minuscule representation in football, maybe 5 percent. There's the example of Becky Hammond coaching in the NBA and the odd female working in the NFL (mainly on special teams), but such a lack of recognition and opportunity in the world's three biggest sports is shameful.

Examine any high-pressure situation—in aviation, banking, the armed forces, surgery, teaching, the legal profession—and there will be significant female representation. Despite exceptions in sports science and physiotherapy, coaching is largely a man's world. I can't wrap my head around that being the case in modern, industrialized, and progressive countries. Why would any business marginalize such a huge talent base, spread across half the world's population? It makes no sense, regardless of the moral case for female empowerment.

Dealing with those who want to treat us like scullery maids is a depressingly regular experience. To give an example, I was sitting back and relaxing in the car taking me up to Manchester for Soccer Aid when the driver, wanting to make conversation, started telling me about a radio show talking about "some bird" during a debate about the capacity of a woman to coach in the ego-driven, money-laden environment of the Premier League. The driver asked me if I knew the "bird" he was talking about.

I had been told I was mentioned on that show, and simply said, "I am her."

The driver quickly backtracked, saying he didn't agree with the tone of the debate, but couldn't help giving his curiosity away. "Can you coach, then?" he asked. "Well, I am the current world coach of the year," I replied, a reference to my Best FIFA Women's Coach Award of 2021.

I was immediately irritated with myself, rising to the bait like that, but sod it. I had to make a point. This bias, this misogyny and sexism, is so deeply rooted in our society it must be called out. A woman in a position of authority needs to be seen in order to prove progress can be made.

There are daily doses of double standards. Why aren't football coaches given the respect afforded to female teachers?

We are both nurturers with specialized skills. Perhaps it is another aspect of the flight-deck experience. Everyone who gets on a plane assumes the pilot is male, but if a female voice comes over the intercom, the knee-jerk reaction is, "Ooh, can she fly this thing?"

Visual representation is gradually improving, even if that means my mug shot illustrating a breaking news story, but myths are allowed to flourish. My job is the same as that of a man in a similar position. We coach human beings. We deliver instruction and supervise teaching.

Yet, in the eyes of the vast majority of the football world, there is zero chance of me managing Chelsea's Premier League team. Apparently, I couldn't handle big characters and the whims of multimillionaires, let alone deal with players wandering around with their willies hanging out.

A word in your ear, boys. I've seen the dangly bits of most of the men who work with me. I didn't run screaming from the room, rustling my crinolines. Come into my dressing room and you will see breasts and vaginas. So what? The human form is central to sport. Get over yourselves.

Oh, and if you want to talk about big characters, the likes of Sam Kerr and Pernille Harder aren't exactly backward in coming forward.

There is a range of challenges within the genders. There's more passive aggression on the women's side, although it is not unusual for me to be confronted more directly. In the men's game you learn to deal with inflated egos and the distorting effect of silly money, which some find difficult to handle. If you are on the receiving end of ignorant assumption of your inferiority in any area of life, the natural reaction is frustration and bafflement. I don't let such attitudes erode my sense of self-worth, so my immediate response is usually "Are you for real?"

I hear some comments and think, what went wrong with the women in your life? I'll be as frank and as clear as I can because I know this will get some people's back up. In a world where so much has changed for men, is football the last thing they have that is theirs, and only theirs?

I'm a mad football fan. I've grown up on the terraces listening to the bile. It can be a very hostile environment. I've run away from fights, and I've had to avoid flares lobbed at us from rival fans. I've done the whole thing. I've been in it. I get it.

I understand the culture. It's a traditional male release at the end of the working week. There's almost a fear that if they let go of football, they're screwed. It is as if they haven't noticed the crowds have changed and have become more diverse. It's ridiculous. We need each other in all walks of life. Why are we so divisive about it?

It worries me that we are so unaware of our biases. It is going to take a profound amount of work and the passage of time to change that. Consistent and persistent education is the key, at home and in the workplace. That's why the Black Lives Matter movement is so important and instructive in combating inherent racism. Very few people admit to being racist. Are we comfortable accepting that at face value?

Someone's son, husband, or brother is that supermarket security guard, following a shopper around because he or she is Black. Someone's daughter, wife, or sister is that mum who crosses the road to avoid contact with someone of different color outside the school gates. When you hear of something like that, or experience it directly, you instinctively recoil, but you need to be sufficiently open-minded and socially aware to appreciate that this is a result of years of conditioning.

Consider sexism from a football perspective. Previous generations have grown up with male commentators, male pundits, male players, male referees, and male coaches. No wonder there is a sense the men's game is for men.

I don't expect significant change until the end of this decade, but a new generation is coming from a different starting point. I appreciate my son Harry is growing up in a distinctive household, but he didn't differentiate between watching my team on Sky TV on Sunday night and the men's team on Monday night. In fact, when he is watching Chelsea's men, he invariably asked, "Why aren't you on the touchline, Mummy?" Bless.

There is far greater exposure to women's sport on TV now. Female commentators and pundits are insightful and impeccably researched. I was blown away by the impact of going on to ITV's Euro 2020 commentary team. I wanted the viewer to see through my eyes, as a coach. My TV work is enjoyable because I get treated like the top football players do. It's not bad being pampered once in a while. I think without my ability to connect and communicate, I wouldn't be where I am today. A coach and leader, or TV pundit for that matter, must convey occasionally complex messages in simple terms. You'd be surprised by how difficult that can be. People take time to understand, so you have to think laterally to get the message across.

I didn't feel I was doing anything out of the ordinary when I started working with ITV, yet it was received as if I had blown up the narrative on how to co-commentate. Both *Broadcast* magazine and the Sports Journalists' Association awarded me the Pundit of the Year prize in 2021. That wasn't intentional, and I certainly didn't expect to start winning awards. Hopefully, I've opened the door for others to walk through.

A female leader of any successful team, whether in sport or in business, is so powerful because it helps to normalize the conversation. I was hugely encouraged at Soccer Aid, where I asked one of my assistants who was standing behind the dugout to take a picture of David Beckham for me.

Old habits die hard.

There were four girls nearby no more than ten years old. They called out to me, "Are you Sam Kerr's coach?" When I said I was, they asked for a photo with me. They knew everything about Sam. They didn't know who Jamie Carragher—the former Liverpool and England player who has become a prominent TV pundit—was when he walked by. I've nothing against Jamie, incidentally, even though I jokingly told him not to bore me when he challenged me during a training session. If I'm using my profile and my players are being appreciated, we are winning off the pitch as well as on it.

There are perks. As a Take That fan growing up, I was privately beside myself to work with former member Robbie Williams at Soccer Aid. He's a fascinating character from a manic world, and I began to understand the vulnerabilities of the man, as opposed to the pop legend. To use the British vernacular, I still managed to blag a photo for my sisters, though.

Getting back to the serious stuff, in the men's game people often become football managers on the strength of their playing careers and without having management experience. What the hell? We're talking about managing people, managing lives, and managing expectations. Why are former football players automatically supposed to make good managers? Do former big spenders become bankers? Do former patients develop into doctors? Do regular airline passengers progress to being pilots? Where does that conceit come from? When are we going to see football coaching as a profession that requires the same skill acquisition as a lawyer, doctor, or brain surgeon?

I really struggle with the myth that only those who have played the game have the secret knowledge. There's no denying a former forward will help one of the strikers improve their finishing, but is he equipped to deal with a death in the family, that player's sexuality, learning disability, or mental health problem? What is there on his résumé to suggest he can help a player handle the onset of illness, the isolation of injury, or an inability to be social and cooperate with others? That's part of the skill set. Without a professional underpinning he will struggle to survive. Instead, having a name gets you fast-tracked because there is no uniformity in the system. That's filtered down from FIFA and through the FA. The governing body lacks a methodological approach to teaching football. It's a free-for-all. Successful industries have structure and sustainability.

I'm almost always the only woman attending coaching courses, and sometimes the sessions make me giggle. I watched one former Premier League player lead an individual session in front of the group, and he was awful. Yet when he came back into the backslapping circle of blokes, he told them he'd smashed it.

It was only when they had melted away that he asked me, quietly, what I thought. Until that point the laddish bravado had been off the scale. After checking that he really wanted feedback rather than false validation, I told him I felt he had lost control of his group. He had a good manner but went on too long. To his credit, he accepted my observations as fair.

Get Your Methodology Right

Want to be a leader in your organization? What processes do you have in place to make sure you meet your people's expectations and they meet yours? Perhaps you don't have a lot of experience in managing human beings, so what's your plan for making them tick? Whether you lead a football club, an advertising agency, or a marketing department, and whatever the dominant generation or sex of your workforce, are you teaching them how to ask for and accept support and how to analyze feedback, or are you just moaning about what they're not doing right?

There is a reason Pep Guardiola is regarded as the best in his field. He has developed a huge underpinning of methodological information. It is a similar story with great contemporary coaches like Jose Mourinho and Jurgen Klopp. The vast majority of coaches at club level fly by the seat of their pants. Bumpy landings are inevitable.

As a leader, ask yourself what defines a professional. It obviously involves more than simply being paid to do a job. You have to be able to communicate your ideas effectively and promote a team ethic. It helps to be altruistic and emotionally intelligent. You must be a clear, critical thinker. Above all, you have to value people and consider others' needs before your own.

That brings us nicely to the question I am bored of answering: why don't you coach in men's football? It's not quite as simple as it appears. Could I do it? Without a shadow of doubt. Would I do it? That depends on the nature of the opportunity.

It has become a tedious little game. An unfamiliar face turns up at the press conference. He tells me he is looking forward to our next match and flatters me that I've achieved everything in the women's game. So, he asks, is this the right time for me to move into men's football?

Here we go again.

I tend to reply, "Do you want a headline? Is this what it's all about? Something to get you through the day? Do we honestly have to have this conversation again?" I'll then rattle off an empty answer, and he will remain ignorant of my true thoughts and intentions.

Actually, I have had several interesting offers. I rejected an approach by a Championship club in England because it coincided with the upheaval of Chelsea's change of ownership. I could not, in good conscience, walk away from my team when they needed me most. I could not add to the chaos created by such uncertainty. One lower league club offered me an unfeasibly large salary, but I turned them down when it became clear they needed me to build the club from the bottom up while simultaneously assembling and coaching a promotion-winning team.

I was headhunted for a reason. They needed someone to look beyond the now. I would have effectively been CEO, technical director, team manager, and head coach. Fortunately, I've been around long enough to listen to that familiar inner voice: "Jack-of-all-trades, master of none. We know how this goes, don't we, Em?" I would have been diverted by the search for a new training ground, schmoozing the local council, or demanding the removal of pigeon poo from season ticket holders' seats. I would have spent most nights scouting because recruitment is critical at every level of the game.

Choose Your Opportunities Wisely

A top professional in any field must never dilute their talent. There are only so many hours in the day and so many strands of working life you can weave together. However tantalizing the opportunity, remind yourself what you are good at and why you are where you are.

Pep Guardiola doesn't spend his time worrying about Manchester City's next satellite club or how many changing rooms the Academy complex needs. Like me, he is in his element on the grass every day, helping athletes to make marginal, yet cumulative, improvements.

The scale of the challenge wasn't the issue. But if I am to break the glass ceiling, I must ensure those following me are not showered by shards.

The first female manager in the top tiers of English men's football will have to get used to ridiculous comments. She will be told that dealing with a high net worth individual like a Premier League player is somehow a greater challenge than dealing with a pregnant woman or an emerging player with an eating disorder. She will be judged by unrealistic standards. I'm exaggerating for effect, but in order to be considered a success, she will be expected by the fans to win each match by a cricket score and win the Champions League in her second season.

That woman will have to be aligned to the right club, the right ownership, the right strategy, and the right structure. Everything will have to be perfect or have been developed from within. Logic suggests the pioneer may well have worked her way up from the Academy. She will know the club, the culture, and the players.

I'm not ruling myself out from making that leap of faith, but I'll tell you one thing: I will not do it until and unless I am convinced everything is in place to give me the best chance of making a go of it. We can all talk a fabulous game, but a thoughtless, over optimistic decision would be career ending. It's lonely enough at the top without having to watch the vultures on the wire waiting for their next meal.

Prominent women in any management field are role models. Keep these pointers in mind:

- Pave the way for the next generation.
- Get your methodology right.
- Choose your opportunities wisely.

Chapter 15

Brain Game

One of the toughest weeks of my life was almost at an end. I felt a failure, even though I had been through a period of intense learning. Sleep-deprived, I was exhausted mentally and emotionally spent.

It had been my first week away ever from Harry, who was eleven months old at the time. I could not wait to see him but I had to complete the formalities of my first coach development course in a couple of years, at the Red Bull complex in Leipzig, Germany.

I was fragile, to say the least, and exceptionally tired despite the nutritional plan, overseen by course director Raymond Verheijen, that provided us with plenty of brain food such as oily fish and the right proteins.

Participants were asked to go to the front of the room and tell our fellow coaches what we had taken from the week. For me, everything was about emotional control. I had a packet of tissues in my hand and stood in the middle of two reference boards, which were there for me to list my unconscious and conscious thoughts.

Practice Mindfulness

I was inspired by Sigmund Freud's concept of the mind as an iceberg with so much hidden beneath the surface. The unconscious mind is a whirlpool of negativity. It contains repressed feelings, hidden thoughts, desires, dreams, and bad memories that are outside of our awareness. It can lead to compulsive, self-defeating behavior through the transmission of fear, anxiety, anger, and prejudice.

The conscious mind contains everything we are aware of at any given moment. It enables us to talk rationally about thoughts, wishes, and emotions. It is a source of enrichment. You might be listening to a piece of music or a conversation; sensations and perceptions pass through your mind, and into the outside world.

To put it in very simple terms, imagine you have a chocolate digestive biscuit in one hand and an orange in the other. Naturally, you want to eat the chocolate biscuit. It is an unconscious thought that comes into your mind. You can't do anything about it.

The conscious brain acts as a protective ring. It tells you to eat the orange because it is better for you. The more you develop your conscious brain, the better your decisions, both in quality and quantity. You have to get in the way of those unconscious urges.

You can train your mind to become more aware of your present reality and less focused on your unconscious thoughts, which are usually oriented around past events or future worries. This is mindfulness: what is going on around you right now, and what your senses are telling you. What can you see, hear, feel? Think of your thoughts as clouds that come and go.

Just observe them and let them float away rather than allowing yourself to be emotionally triggered by them.

My initial aim was to stimulate my unconscious mind, deep below Freud's symbolic waterline. I thought about Harry and about how much I missed him. As I did so, I felt myself filling up. I could sense the discomfort of everyone around me.

Tears were soon streaming down my face. I was conscious of their impact but didn't want them to get in the way of how I was feeling. I needed to let everything flow, literally and metaphorically. The atmosphere was awkward. The room was completely silent. As I moved across to the board that represented my conscious mind, my thoughts and demeanor changed. I started to describe the tissues. I talked about their texture and absorbency, how they felt in my hand and on my skin. I described the packaging and labeling in detail. I recalled where I had found them. In making those descriptions in a matter-of-fact manner, I had moved from the emotional to the rational part of my brain. I was no longer getting in my own way.

I then shifted across to the unconscious board and wrote down how many days I had been away from Harry. I described what I missed most about him: his smell, his cuddles, his laughter, and his love. Sure enough, the tears came again, in floods.

More discomfort and shuffling in the seats.

I returned to the conscious board and wrote down my first-choice team, calmly and deliberately. I put it into a 4-4-2 formation but moved the parts around to encompass different passages of play. I spoke about challenging players by developing their roles and defining their personalities.

This wasn't the usual dry, analytical prematch brief. The subtext was obvious. My conscious brain had reestablished control of the conversation. I had proved we think at two levels. Rational, conscious thinking is a variable that comes and goes. In certain situations, it can complement deeply felt emotions.

Encourage Lateral Thinking

Freud employed dream analysis and the sharing of seemingly random thoughts to bring true feelings to light. It is fair to say Raymond Verheijen uses rather more direct methods to usher his pupils toward self-enlightenment. To say he is Marmite Man, loved and loathed in equal measure, is an understatement. It has been reported that Raymond has fallen out spectacularly with the likes of Jurgen Klopp, Arsène Wenger, Mauricio Pochettino, and Jose Mourinho after claiming they were pushing their players too hard physically. Phil Neville, when challenged as manager of England women's team, called him "a keyboard warrior."

Raymond has that Dutch trait of being waspish, a little arrogant, and unconcerned by criticism. He has worked at the highest level as an assistant to Guus Hiddink in South Korea and Russia, and alongside Louis Van Gaal at Barcelona. His résumé also includes stints with Manchester City and the Welsh national team.

In my view, a leader should not shy away from working with an iconoclast, providing that their attacks on cherished principles, personalities, or institutions are based on solid reasoning and authentic experience (which Raymond's are). The mavericks that you invite to your organization can assist a leader by encouraging people to think more laterally, recalibrating the comfort zone in team-building exercises, and suggesting better systems. It takes courage to give an expert with a left field approach the floor, so choose them wisely.

Raymond began as an expert on football fitness and physical conditioning, but over a period of time he has worked extensively around training loads for teams to reduce injuries and enhance performance. I first became aware of him in late 2005, when I was head soccer coach of Iona College, a Roman Catholic university in New Rochelle, New York.

His work was painfully relevant since two of my players had ruptured knee ligaments in the space of a week. One, a lovely girl named Janey Reid, destroyed all four main ligaments—the anterior cruciate, posterior cruciate, medial collateral, and lateral collateral. I was sitting by the pitch and heard them go one by one. Ping, ping, ping, ping. The noise was somehow sinister and reverberated around me. It was the sound of a career ending. I was devastated and angered on her behalf.

Working in the college game in the US, we became used to playing every Friday and Sunday in a truncated but relentless season lasting from August to the end of November. For someone used to the rhythms and demands of English football, it was an alien environment. Injuries were very common. The same sentence always accompanied them: "Oh, she was just terribly unlucky." I sat there and thought to myself, I cannot accept that answer. I cannot accept these are unhappy accidents. So many of the injuries came not from tackles but from fatigue.

Then I read about this guy Verheijen, who had developed the periodization model mentioned previously, a tailored strategy to avoid the stressors that lead to injuries. I knew nothing about it, or him, but saw he was running a six-week single-day course at Wolverhampton Wanderers FC. It suited my schedule perfectly, since I had agreed to return to London to assist Vic Akers at Arsenal FC from the start of the 2006–2007 season.

I was the only woman attending the course, as usual, and was assigned to partner the late Wales manager Gary Speed, whose loss is still keenly felt. The coaching directors of all the national associations were in the cohort, together with senior coaches, some of whom had incredible track records.

Raymond set the tone in his opening address: "I want you to know that everything you do and everything you teach is absolute shite." Instantly the room woke up. I quickly learned that this was business as usual; Raymond liked to trigger brains with bold statements.

He was speaking my language. Like many, I had been terribly disappointed in the formal coach education from the governing bodies. I felt that particularly keenly, since mentions of the women's game were nonexistent in the syllabus. There was zilch, nothing, nada.

The standard teaching process was around phases of play, passing patterns, and buildups in 8-on-8 sessions. I would always come away feeling so let down by the lack of reference to real things that happened regularly in my world.

How do you train? How long do you train for? How do you manage the loading on each player? What is the right preparation for a match, to ensure optimal effectiveness? All these questions that popped up quite naturally and normally were never answered.

So, when Raymond punched the lights out of the governing bodies, he was introducing me to the art of possibilities. Some of the bigwigs in the course with delicate egos didn't like it and drifted away at lunchtime, but I loved it. It was a hallelujah moment. He started to teach us a framework, considerations to work around. His starting point was keeping our players on the pitch. He guided us through the working week, taking into account different game days.

His rules were not for idle discussion. There would be no massively intense sessions seventy-two hours before a game. The proper recovery period after a game, he said, was forty-eight hours. He rationalized these restraints by relating it to getting your car out of the garage for the first time after you've been away. It's a bit cold, and the engine needs time to warm up. In football, where you were told to do intensive training sessions at the start of the week, we were expected to hit top gear straight away. None of us had been taught there was another way.

Those six weeks opened my eyes. Raymond was extremely direct, incredibly challenging. He demanded nothing other than your full attention and focus. As far as he was concerned coaching courses were a glorified coffee club.

I knew what he meant. On previous courses I'd attended the tutors would say, "We will have an hour and then we'll break. Then we'll have lunch and leave at 4." It was all a bit too cozy, too chummy, and comfortable. In Raymond's world you are there for the entirety. None of this half-day nonsense.

If you are planning on only being there for two of the three days, don't bother coming. If you are late, leave and don't come back. Certainly, whatever you do, do not let your mobile phone ring.

Raymond wants to re-create a dressing room environment, which, with its simmering tensions, is not for the fainthearted. There is considerable value in being reminded of the nature of our world. I am always on edge when I attend his sessions. It took me a long time to work out that his confrontational style was deliberate.

He has subsequently developed his teaching from the physical to the mental, with a concept he calls braining. This encapsulates his logic that we often treat the brain as something different instead of it being just another muscle, something to be strengthened and developed as we do with the rest. His starting point was how we strengthen the brain as muscle in a football context.

I found it directly applicable. To give an example involving my Chelsea team, how can I help a young, hugely talented player like Lauren James approach a game knowing she is going to get the life kicked out of her because of the threat she represents? I purposely try to send her over the edge in her preparations, by ensuring decisions are biased against her. Foul tackles are not punished. She discovers how to sustain defiance in the face of provocation, despite being infuriated.

Raymond has written extensively on the implication of overloading the brain with competing demands. He is a philosopher and a scientist—a mad scientist at that. He uses the principles of human evolution as an objective reference to demonstrate how players should be coached and fills the void left by traditional courses, which fail to outline a methodological approach to how you train the brain. By exploring the difference between objective knowledge and subjective experiences, he helps to ensure your coaching is based on trusted facts rather than the latest football fad.

I have spent the last fifteen years of my career asking myself how I apply such knowledge. What does it look like with the women I am working with and representing every day? Are there differences in the brain between men and women? If so, what are they? This, remember, is in addition to the issues around our menstrual cycle and other physiological traits specific to women.

My experience tells me that the female brain is wired differently, especially toward social networks. As a result of that, it isn't just about being *the* best. There are other factors involved in making a team work, most notably in how a player can help a colleague exude confidence and happiness.

I appreciate that this sounds a little silly, but there is a bit of a problem when we go on away trips because we stay in the hotels used by the men's team. They tend to be in the middle of nowhere. That doesn't really matter because the guys will play FIFA video games in their rooms. Women are more social. We want to go to the coffee shop, to sit and have a chat.

Most of us don't want to play on our computers, so as a leader I have to create a suitable environment. Building connections is valuable to us, and for us. The group believes it is important we go for dinner together after games, when the sports scientists would say we'd be better going home and getting more sleep. It is important we give time to one another because camaraderie and teamwork go hand in hand.

The sexes process neurochemicals differently. Women have lower levels of serotonin, which carries messages between nerve cells in the brain and throughout the body. Since serotonin influences body functions such as mood, sleep, digestion, and nausea, it follows that females are more prone to anxiety. On the other hand, we have better reading comprehension and writing ability and are more intuitive thinkers.

Our fine-motor coordination skills are more effective, and our speed of perception is quicker. Women are also more adept at retrieving information from our long-term memories. I was particularly intrigued by a study of rhesus monkeys. The males preferred toys with wheels; the females took a liking to soft toys. Since I have a son who loves trains, not to mention gooey plastic poo, I can relate to that.

Internally, at Chelsea, we were very aware of neuroscience, but there are so many parallels across the working world. I have to be aware of the unconscious biases of my coaches, my middle-management equivalents. Do they influence the actions of a particular individual?

As a leader, I watch out for anchoring bias, the individual who is reliant on the first piece of information she hears. Think about it in a wider context: whoever makes the first offer in a salary negotiation establishes a range of reasonable possibilities in each person's mind.

Some people overestimate the relevance of the information that is available to them. They might argue that smoking is not unhealthy, simply because they know someone who got through twenty cigarettes a day and lived to be a hundred years old.

The bandwagon effect—people adopting the opinions of those around them—often makes meetings unproductive. We live in an era that many have characterized as "cancel culture." Some leaders are wary of sharing their real opinions with younger members of staff in case they are seen as out of touch or ideologically unacceptable to them.

Consider ways that you can foster a more open dialogue that crosses the divide. People recognize cognitive and motivational biases more readily in others than in themselves. Leaders must beware of double standards. Practice what you preach.

Remember also that when you take the initiative and choose something you tend to feel positive about it, even it has obvious flaws. You'll love your dog, for instance, even if it nips a stranger every once in a while.

Beware of seeing patterns in random events. That underpins various gambling fallacies, like the notion red is more likely to turn up in roulette after a string of reds. In my world, winning streaks are an illusion, as is the idea you should blindly continue to give the ball to a player who is playing really well. We tend to listen only to what we want, especially if we are trying to make decisions with a tired brain. That takes me back to the course in Leipzig, which remains the most brain-intensive exercise I have ever undertaken.

Graham Potter, my former Chelsea colleague who was then managing Brighton, was put into the top set of four. I was allocated the bottom set. That was a deliberate act on Raymond's part, because he wanted to see how I coped with coaches who had different knowledge, backgrounds, and experiences than mine.

They did not work at the level to which Graham and I were accustomed. One was from an Under-12 boys team in Hong Kong, another from the Dutch Under-16s. The third was in the American system. We were all existing on three hours' sleep a night and were expected to start preparing presentations at midnight for the following morning.

I don't want to belittle those colleagues in any way. They had a fascination with the process and had total commitment to learning. Our thirty-minute collective presentation was around our theoretical understanding of situational coaching, something that no one really understood, even though the basic principle—the need to balance imparting knowledge versus allowing the player to discover it for themselves through the experience of certain situations—is relatively straightforward.

In that situation, misunderstandings create misalignment and miscommunications, irritation, and agitation. Everyone had a different definition of our task. Everyone's language was different. Remember the Tower of Babel with the 800 different channels, which I spoke of in a previous chapter? This was it, brought to life.

Raymond knew I was missing Harry. I couldn't cope without my child. I'd been sobbing during the reference boards exercise. I hated being away from him. I wanted to go home but knew I could not quit. I was failing miserably and struggled to comprehend conflicting emotions.

At the end of the second day, Raymond called me up to the front of the room. He simply said, "Emma, tell me how you are feeling." I left him no room for doubt. We started each day at 8:00 a.m. He had offered me the chance to come later, so I'd have a little more sleep and be fresher for the sessions. I said no. Predictably, the following morning, I overslept. The group had already left to go to the training pitches in Leipzig.

I had to walk all the way there because I couldn't get a cab. I swear to God, I have never eaten so much humble pie in my life. As I walked in, Raymond was delivering a session with the Leipzig Under-18s. I saw him look at me, but he said nothing until we went back into the classroom later that afternoon. He sat down and, much like he does to all of us, said, "Emma, you have a choice to make. Get better or go home."

I yearned to go home. I was desperate to get back to my boy. I was battling myself. He was explicitly challenging me. But no matter how impressive your track record, no matter how talented people think you are, you cannot let people down in a team environment. So I went to my room and wrote a note to him, outlining my commitment for the following five days of the course. I was staying. I knew I had to lose myself in the process to get the most out of the experience and to prove to myself that I had the requisite staying power. From that point on I immersed myself in learning in a way I had never done before.

Stay Measured When Under Pressure

During the course, Raymond asked us to think of a situation that triggered unbelievable fear. I summoned the image of walking down a long dark alley, which brings out feelings of terror in me. To me, that is a different fear, for example, than jumping out of an airplane, in which the danger would feel exhilarating. It begged the question: How can people under extreme pressure, experiencing the most intense stress, make optimal decisions in life and death situations?

Raymond used the example of a soldier coming under fire while walking through a minefield. You had better walk in the footsteps of the person in front of you without a pause in your focus. The minute you stop to think about something else, like your family back at home, you are dead. The minute you stop to think about how hungry and tired you are, and how you would love to lie down, it is over. If you hear the first gunshot and begin thinking I am going to die, you are more likely to do so. If you go back to your processes, and think *rifle, return fire,* you have a greater chance of surviving. You are either going to manage information logically, despite your nervous system being in an uproar, or you are going to succumb to your fears.

That coaching course in Germany was such a wake-up call for me. I finally understood the importance of emotional control. I reaffirmed the significance of my body language. Matches have manager cams, looking for every twitch made during a game. My players, both on the pitch and on the bench, will be studying me and trying to read what I'm thinking.

I have to be at the front of my brain all the time, meaning I need to maintain absolute focus without responding to emotional triggers. I have to make measured decisions. No one is going to die, but we are going to win or lose. Recognizing when I am in an emotional state and how to get out of it is critical.

As leaders, our people are watching us. As parents, our children are watching us. Developing control over your emotional responses is key in both scenarios. Teaching is an unconscious exchange—if you don't feel you're in charge, chances are you've already lost your players, colleagues, or students. Developing a strong belief in your authority is vital, especially when mistakes have been made, and staying in your conscious mind will keep you grounded.

That's all very well, I hear you say, but what has that got to do with my world? All I can say is that however narrow my objectives as a football coach are, we are all vulnerable to acts of fate—events that come at us with no warning.

As I was talking through this passage of the book with Mike, my cowriter, I heard Harry cry. I dashed into his playroom and found blood on his head. He had been so engrossed with his trains he had walked into a cupboard door. My initial response was *I can't breathe, it's my child, he's hurting.* Then I engaged my conscious mind, sat down with him, comforted him, and calmly looked at the cut. This enabled me to reestablish control.

It took me back to another crisis point: the day Harry had a seizure. Oh my God. We were getting ready to go to the US, where I was due to serve as a commentator on ESPN. He was sitting with his cousin Isabella in the living room. I was upstairs, on the top floor, helping mum with washing.

Isabella ran to the top of the stairs and blurted out: "Harry is doing something strange." I flew down the stairs to find Harry on the sofa having seizures. Understandably, everyone in the room was screaming. I picked him up and instantly realized he was in a bad way. I didn't know what to do.

My parents were paralyzed. My unconscious brain was doing its worst. Was he going to die? I instantly forced myself into a conscious mindset and asked my sister to call 999, the emergency number. I turned him on his side, checked his tongue, and tried to talk to him.

"Can you hear me, Harry?"

Think, think, think. Paramedics came on the phone and said the ambulance would be an hour. I had a split-second decision to make. Do I wait or get him to hospital under our own steam? I chose our car.

I scooped him up, laid him in the recovery position on the back seat, opened the windows and sat beside him, talking constantly, while my sister drove us to the hospital. I kept calm. I'm not saying I wasn't fearful and terrified, but that was something to be acknowledged later. This was about the here and now.

It's no different to anyone, in any walk of life, confronting a crisis. Do they freeze or do they respond by taking rational steps? My communication with the professionals concerned had to be clear. I had to deal with my fear and frustrations. Mercifully, Harry recovered.

Over time, I have learned to think clearly under pressure. The amygdala area of our brain can hijack our fight-or-flight response, making the prospect of even routine events such as public speaking engagements or chairing meetings a trigger for panic. Try Raymond's exercise with colleagues using the reference boards.

The simplest way to explain it is you have to get in the way of your fears. I still have panicky moments, particularly when they are related to family, but I've learned to intervene in these moments. Talking yourself down from the scariest of places isn't easy, but it is necessary. Here are some tips to keep in mind:

- Practice mindfulness.
- Encourage lateral thinking.
- Stay measured when under pressure.

Chapter 16

Human Soup

We live in a world of boomers and Zoomers, X's and Y's. Somehow, we have to make that human soup created by the crossover of successive generations in the workplace nourishing, flavorful, and fulfilling. It is a difficult job, but a decisive factor in so many organizations.

I stand by the principle that a leader had better know themselves before they analyze anyone else. I was born in October 1976, toward the tail end of Generation X, which is classified as those individuals born between 1965 and 1980. I can recognize some of the traditional characteristics of that group, which tends to be well-educated, self-reliant, and confident with autonomy. Yet I also identify with the competitiveness and work ethic of the previous generation, the baby boomers. Accomplishment is important to me.

By and large, my staff and players at Chelsea straddled the millennial and Zoomer generations, also known as Y and Z. Paul Green, my general manager, is the same age as me. My principal coaches, Denise Reddy, Tanya Oxtoby, and Stuart Searle are ages fifty-two, forty, and forty-three, respectively. In terms of age, that's a fairly standard cross section of coaching teams across professional sport. Our common challenge is to relate to our athletes by appreciating modern lifestyle priorities and understanding the dynamics of peer group pressure. The contradictions are stark, but comparisons require subtlety.

Zoomers, those under the age of twenty-six, are generally more socially responsible, but want both stability and flexibility, which is hard to reconcile. Millennials, my more senior players, value feedback and respond to more meaningful work. They are perceived as being less loyal yet respond to a collaborative approach.

How do we coach and manage this hybrid group in a hugely competitive environment? With the proviso that not everyone conforms to these stereotypes and that elite sport demands certain nonnegotiable qualities, supposedly typical cultural traits provide obvious challenges.

Speaking generally, millennials and Zoomers don't want to work as hard as we were expected to when we were making our way up. That doesn't make it wrong, but it is another variable we have to consider. They place greater importance on a better work-life balance, but because they often have abbreviated attention spans due to the overwhelming impact of the internet and rapidly evolving social media channels, information has to be condensed into bite-size chunks to be absorbed.

Some of them would probably prefer an app that allows them to digest highlights and a summary of a book in fifteen minutes rather than read the book itself. Instead of committing to the process of self-education they're more interested in being told what lessons it contains so they can put them into operation right away. They have an instinct for cutting corners, and look for the quickest, easiest route to the top. Their ambition is off the scale, despite the gnawing doubts generated by impostor syndrome.

Reach Out to the Dopamine Generation

Social media has altered the way our minds work. My players are constantly watching what people are saying about them. It dictates their behavior. Depending on the nature of their online narrative, they come to me for advice or a good old-fashioned argument.

I am trying to teach them that responsibility to the team is the essence of professionalism. Acceptance of the collective importance of the group is often at odds with their self-image, especially if I have to make difficult selection decisions.

Their emotional response to being dropped is understandable, when you consider that people they will never meet are telling them they are amazing. Sometimes they are affronted by the reality I represent. When I do not play them, I might be accused of devaluing their brand and affecting their social status.

Those messages are amplified by that other modern phenomenon, the entourage, which includes families and, inevitably, agents. They think nothing of swooping down like avenging angels on Facebook, Instagram, and X (formerly Twitter) to express their outrage on their player's behalf.

Some even use their mobile phone for what it was originally intended, to call me to complain. It's white noise. Put politely, sometimes it is tempting to tell the lot of them to go away. But can I be so direct, and to the point? My God, no. I am expected to empathize even if the poses struck are occasionally absurd.

Players may become consumed by impatience, have a compulsion to share their feelings on social media, and lack reliable coping mechanisms. That's why, in my world, the introduction of coachability coaches to help players to work with constructive criticism would be as valuable—if not more valuable—than conventional roles such as nutritionists or psychologists.

People seem to find it harder to take instructions nowadays. The issues that affect this generation are as relevant in any modern office environment as they are on my training ground. Instead of accepting instruction, some players will retreat online, where outlets promote the seductive myth that they know it all.

What I see is a flawed but talented individual who needs help. They see this hologram of perfection, an idealistic version of themselves, reflected back at them. They cannot digest constructive feedback because they prefer to concentrate on the views of an online army of followers, people who have no conception of who the player is and what they do. This can also fuel insecurities because the gulf between their artificially presented external image and their true inner self appears to widen.

Tough love has its merits.

In recent years, educationalists have focused more on the celebration of children taking part in sports events at school rather than on encouraging individuals to win trophies. Best of luck if you expect praise for finishing last or any other objective measure of failure in the real world. Some primary schools now offer medals on a collective basis; in general, however, an anticompetitive culture invites underachievement and, ultimately, frustration.

Our problem is the availability of the most natural of drugs, dopamine, which is triggered by the affirmations of social media. A chemical released by the brain, dopamine enables you to feel pleasure, satisfaction, and stimulates a sense of urgency. Too little of it, and your mood dips. You become anxious, prone to depression.

Imagine injecting such a substance into your veins. It would be so easy to veer between fulfillment and fear. If dopamine was sold on the streets, it would be subject to legislation. A mobile phone can be deadly because it is a dopamine decider. It is the drug pusher in plain sight. Want a hit? Count your likes and retweets. Do a funny dance on TikTok and wait for the LOLs and the smiley emojis to roll in.

But beware the bad trip. Someone on X tells you that you're ugly and useless. Other users pile on, gleefully increasing your misery. It is the modern equivalent of being locked in the stocks and pelted with rotten tomatoes.

The current generation does not know how to react to this. They struggle to channel powerful feelings. I have lost count of the number of passive-aggressive tweets posted by athletes in adversity that have made me wince. They are unwitting cries for help.

I understand the game. It doesn't matter to me whether you think I am the best thing in the world or the worst. I am aware of the irrationality of the extremes, so it isn't going to affect me. I am fortunate that I was brought up in a generation that understands how to manage emotion.

Encourage Regular Digital Detoxes

When the Chicago Red Stars sacked me in 2010, I had a barely used one-year-old Twitter account at the time. I had signed up only because I felt it would help me in my duty to promote the women's game. It wasn't my window on the world or a cozy comfort blanket, and I didn't rush to it in search of solace in the aftermath of a very public rejection.

I was on my own, far from home, dealing with failure. For two weeks I had the perspective of silence. I had to live with myself without comment, without guidance. It's a natural process of mourning and reflection. Instead of retreating into myself, I slowly advanced.

That resilience doesn't make me special or unique. Denise Reddy, who left her job with Chicago at the same time, went through something similar. I accepted the sympathies of individuals I knew and respected but didn't need the cheap thrill of support from strangers.

The experience taught me the importance of mindfulness, of sitting by myself and working through thoughts and sensitivities. It disappoints me immensely that so many players do not see the value of meditation. The act of controlling your breath and your brain is enlightening.

It takes time and training, but meditation is actually a performance enhancer if you learn to use it wisely. This might surprise you, but I believe it to be five times more beneficial than a decent night's sleep. Unfortunately, modern life, technologically driven at an ever-faster pace, militates against serenity. Many in the current generation—and, to be fair, some of their elders—simply can't bear the idea of sitting still. That's their choice, their prerogative. Yet they do need to be reminded of the harmful effects of social media. The best players do not linger there for long. The ones who leave social media benefit from the freedom. When they leave the online arena, I get them back as human beings.

It's up to leaders to bring in rules to restrict the use of mobile phones. We all know how addictive they are, and their potential impact on productivity is undeniable. Establish a policy in your workplace and enforce it. This policy should include no phones during meetings, and limitations on social media use during working hours.

Having said that, leaders have to evolve with the times. We must adapt or die, like polar bears that travel for ten hours over melting ice caps to fight among each other for declining stocks of food. We are as vulnerable to fate as those newly born seal cubs, slipping off the splintered pack ice and drowning because they are not ready to swim.

You guessed it. I'm hooked on David Attenborough's documentaries. Most episodes of the *Frozen Planet* are a three-hankie job. Those Arctic animals are going to have to find a way to survive; otherwise, like the panda bears whose habitat is being devastated by deforestation in China, they will decline toward extinction.

Nature is brutal and compelling. It might sound a bit trite to make comparisons, but the one thing I know about performance in any industry is that if you fail to evolve and open your mind to find solutions to sudden challenges, you will die.

So, how do we stir the human soup, so that it simmers nicely?

I try to stimulate a sense of belonging, regardless of the date on your birth certificate. I attempt to work across generations, encouraging individuals to share ideas. Diversity of thought and differences in emphasis are good things when filtered through an open mind. My workforce will never be treated as numbers, although, come to think of it, the players do wear them on their back. That casual disregard of an employee's humanity is a mistake too many corporations make.

Leaders who do not bother to find out who their staff are, and what matters to them, are going through the motions. These staff members are recognizable human beings, contrasting characters with distinctive needs. I will be their most passionate advocate. I will broadcast the impact and importance of their contributions. I promise I will be there for them when things do not go so well. It's a form of marriage vow: for better, for worse, for richer, for poorer.

Conflict is inevitable but retrievable. Clear your lines of communication. Discover the intrinsic motivations of those around you. These are touchstones that can form the foundation of mutually rewarding personal relationships. Speaking of rewards, I am as transparent and collaborative as possible when it comes to the bonus structure for my team. I ask them how they want the money to be distributed and on what scale within the group. I will incorporate their views into the reviews of my staff.

What more do you need from us? How could we do our jobs better? What is the missing link in the coaching, conditioning, or medical departments? What do we need more of or less of? How else can we improve our relationships? If you don't tell us, we will never know.

Prepare for the Next Revolution

We are entering another transformative era. I do not profess to understand the nuances of AI, but there is no question it will be the biggest technological development in terms of the magnitude of its application in the coming years. AI will become the new norm, our new internet. That's both exciting and scary. We're already whispering sweet nothings to Alexa. Hundreds of thousands of robots are processing our online orders for food, clothing, and any other consumer goods you care to imagine.

The pace of change is accelerating. Around a third of UK businesses are making significant investments in automation. Two-thirds of UK businesses fear it will lead to widespread job losses. Computers are working at increasing speed and harvesting huge amounts of data. I use this instinctively at the moment, on the training pitch or in our group analysis sessions, but it is thought that machine learning, language processing, and facial recognition software will eventually gauge the emotions of students to help determine who is struggling or bored. That will certainly add an edge to our dressing room discussions.

The future is rushing toward us. OpenAI, the organization cofounded by Elon Musk, revealed that it taught a computer to read and write in 2019. The organization launched its first commercial product, a rentable text-generation tool—once felt too dangerous to release on the open market—in 2020. Things did not evolve as planned; in March 2024, Musk sued OpenAI for abandoning its original mission for profit. He called AI a "double-edged sword," and supported a campaign for a six-month pause in developing more powerful systems, citing risks to humanity.

The current obsession with ChatGPT, a natural language processing tool driven by AI, was launched on November 30, 2022, and has the potential to be the most significant advance since the internet. It is the fastest growing app of all time and allows you to have humanlike conversations with a chatbot. ChatGPT can answer questions, admit its mistakes, challenge incorrect assumptions, and reject inappropriate requests. It can also assist you in writing emails, essays, and computer code.

We are not all about to be enslaved by androids, but every facet of our lives will be affected. Don't take my word for it. Ask the 352 experts assembled by the grandly titled Future of Humanity Institute at Oxford University. They believe machines will be capable of writing school essays by 2026. Self-driving vehicles will start to be used widely by 2027. AI will have phased most humans out of the retail sector by 2031, and machines will be writing best-selling books by 2049.

Oh, and by 2137, all human jobs will be automated. Let's face it: if a machine can explain the handball laws and offside decisions in football's VAR (video assistant referee) system or come up with a fail-safe tactical method of countering the opposition's pressing strategy, I might as well give up now. I won't, of course, because as a leader I have to navigate change as calmly as I possibly can, in the knowledge that people are inclined to mirror you in every shape or form. I'm used to being watched as a coach and I know, from being a mum, how my child can sense if I am anxious or apprehensive.

It's not just me. Harry felt the nervousness of two female passengers sitting close to us on a bumpy flight home from Orlando, Florida. I explained to him that it was like being on the Tube back in London. You feel the bumps and move up and down with them as you go down the tracks from station to station.

Describe what is happening and it will calm the fears. That's what occurs when the pilot tells passengers in reassuring tones to expect some turbulence along the route. If it happens when you have been prepared for it instead of it manifesting itself unexpectedly, you have calmer passengers instead of everyone freaking out.

We must never lose that human touch, since perhaps the greatest threat represented by AI is the way it highlights and promotes homogenous skills and attitudes. If everything or everyone is the same, it will lead to a reduction in innovation, creativity, and flexibility.

When it comes down to it, I believe in people rather than machines, regardless of age or influences. I can't get my head around businesses that do not consider the benefits of cognitive diversity, which involves an awareness of the variety of ways in which people think.

Gather people around you from a wide range of backgrounds and generations. Encourage them to be themselves. Challenge existing assumptions. Promote new ideas. Look at life through a different lens. Success is not just about talent or experience, it is about having the courage to take off your blinders. Make the most of the opportunities that a multigenerational workforce presents.

To summarize,

- reach out to the "dopamine" generation.
- encourage regular digital detoxes.
- prepare for the next revolution.

Chapter 17

Keep Your Friends Close

We all know the stereotypes, don't we? The preening, scheming, and vengeful alpha male who is willing to trample over everyone and everything to get to the top. The femme fatale in a pencil skirt, high heels, and with a mushroom cloud of Chanel N°5 surrounding her who uses her femininity like a flick knife.

It takes all sorts, I suppose. Football, like many other industries, is a deceptively small world. Certain individuals simply don't care if they acquire a reputation for plotting against their superiors with the aim of eventually replacing them.

I take pride in taking the opposite stance. Competitiveness and compassion are not mutually exclusive. I am quite happy to mentor rival managers and coaches, irrespective of potential competitive disadvantage. Perhaps it's a sign that, at long last, I've grown up.

Nurture Your Friends

In the early phases of my career, I wanted to be known for my football and for my tactical acumen. I wanted the approval of my contemporaries. As I've picked up greater experience and knowledge, I've left that battle behind. I'm determined to be the best version of myself, with the understanding that I will get on better with some people than others.

In any walk of life there will always be those willing to cut you off at the knees to get what they want. The male game, in particular, seems harsh. From what I've seen, their culture encourages emotional immaturity and terminal insecurity.

My message is simple: let me know how I can help. As a leader in a relatively young industry, like women's football, I owe it to others to be empathetic and supportive. It is an extension of my orientation toward the team.

I know I cannot control the perception anyone has of me, whether it is favorable or cynical. All I do know is that being transparent and honest seems to be very rare. I don't want to be remembered as a winner if it means that people will qualify that by thinking I am an arsehole. What I want most of all is to grow the game. There is a lot of inexperience. A lot of good people are literally learning on the job.

I vividly remember when I was in the same boat as an emerging female coach. I have a different relationship with Hope Powell these days, but back then I found it impossible to link up with and learn from her. She was a pioneering, hugely successful figure, but out of reach.

Oh, how I looked up to her. She had translated a stellar playing career, in which she won sixty-six caps for England as an attacking midfield player after making her international debut at age sixteen, into a uniquely influential role as England's first-ever national coach for the women's team. She led the team to four UEFA Championship finals, reached the quarterfinals of the World Cup, and was coach of Team GB at the 2012 Olympics. I related hugely to her background. Like me, she grew up playing on the streets of her council estate.

She defied her mother, who did not want her to play football due to the cultural sensibilities of the West Indian community in which she grew up. She had a keen awareness of the game's potential. Even her name—Hope—seemed significant to me. In addition to managing England's senior team, she oversaw the age-group structure teams up to the Under-23s, established a coach mentoring scheme, and was a key figure in the establishment of the FA's National Development Centre at Loughborough University.

She was the first female coach to earn UEFA's Pro License, our highest qualification. That's an amazing body of work, but, as far as she was concerned, it was as if I didn't exist. As a young coach with a thirst for knowledge that barrier drove me insane. I had no accessible role models until I went to the US, where the women's game was more developed.

I then found a million role models. It was another world in the US. I realized quite quickly that if it was between me and a male counterpart, I was always getting the job, based on merit. That was such a weird feeling, because at the age of twenty-six there was nothing for me in the English system.

Can you imagine the confidence that gave me? I was in an environment that pushed me to achieve my goals. I felt supported, encouraged, and valued. I wasn't treated as an upstart or with a lack of respect.

The warmth of the response had a lasting effect on me. I was influenced by two fabled coaches at the University of North Carolina: Anson Dorrance, whose openness I have already mentioned in this book, and Dean Smith, who spent thirty-six seasons overseeing a legendary basketball program.

When Smith passed away in 2015 at the age of eighty-three, the tributes concentrated not only on the symbols of his success—879 wins, two national championships, and 77.6 winning percentage—but on the impact he had as a human being. Michael Jordan, his most celebrated pupil, described him as "a mentor, my teacher, my second father." Former players spoke of how he cared for them as individuals on and off the court. In his will, he left $200 to every letterman who played for him during his thirty-six seasons. It was a posthumous recognition of the special status afforded valued athletes in the US college system. (A letterman has symbolic importance for meeting specified levels of participation or performance. The term refers to the practice of awarding a cloth letter, usually the school's initial or initials, on a special jacket or sweater.)

Smith adhered to the most important principle of leadership in practicing what he preached. He set personal examples in his punctuality, work ethic, respect for others, and belief in continual learning. He knew when to step in and when to keep out of the way. Reciprocal loyalty underpinned his coaching. It was a cornerstone of the culture he embedded. He was accessible to his athletes and delivered life lessons that had an impact beyond the basketball court. In return for his guidance and commitment, he received his players' respect, deference, and unremitting effort.

Loyalty is a recurring theme in the methodology of great coaches. The legendary John Wooden, who won ten NCAA national men's basketball championships in twelve years at UCLA, insisted it began with loyalty to his standards, system, and personal values. He believed the best leaders both in sports or business understood the deeply personal nature of the connection between them and the athletes or employees under their influence. Wooden said,

> People do not arrive at your doorstep with loyalty. It comes when those you lead see and experience that your concern for their interests and welfare goes beyond simply calculating what they can do for you, how you can use them to your advantage. I believe most people, the overwhelming majority of us, wish to be in an organization whose leadership cares about them, provides fairness and respect, dignity and consideration.
>
> Do so and you will find loyalty in abundance from those you lead. You will find yourself in charge of an organization that will not waffle in the wind. You will find a group of individuals who will stay committed even when things get tough.

Pat Lyons, the first athletic director I worked under, taught me that ambition is not a dirty word. He was twenty-eight, two years older than me when he was my boss at Iona College. I was the head soccer coach, and although the job lacked a little scope, I was in heaven. It remains one of my favorite experiences.

Pat brought me into his office one day to tell me he'd taken a call from someone at St. John's University, a Roman Catholic university in Queens, New York. They wanted to hire me, and it was an obvious step up. Could we talk about it?

To be honest, his request threw me. I was brought up in an environment where people sneaked off for job interviews rather than discussing them with their boss. He asked what I wanted from my career, and what it would take for me to stay where I was.

I couldn't answer immediately because I wasn't used to the transparency of the process. He offered to speak to St. John's on my behalf if that would help me. That blew me away. Supporting any application, even though it would work against him, was a fundamental demonstration of faith.

As it happened, I stayed at Iona for three more years, while Pat left in 2011 for Seton Hall University. In 2019 he was promoted from athletic director to an all-encompassing role as the university president's chief of staff. The kids there did all right.

His openness and generosity of spirit was one of the main reasons I returned to England, determined to mentor others. I know how lonely the coaching journey can be. I'm open to all-comers, beyond my club and dressing room. I have formed special relationships with two other mothers who have managed against me in the Women's Super League, Kelly Chambers at Reading and Carla Ward at Aston Villa. We are bonded by something bigger than ourselves.

I know all too well how working mothers suffer with heightened emotions and fragile confidence. I approached Kelly and Carla with complete honesty: there was no ulterior motive, as there often is in professional sport. Our teams might have been in competition, but on an individual basis I wanted to be their sounding board in those moments when life gets in the way.

I'm grateful I've never had issues with depression. The only time I've really struggled was after I had Harry, dealing with being a manager, a mum, and losing a child at the same time. It wasn't as debilitating as it could have been, but it was really new to me.

Remember Pressure Is a Privilege

Kelly had been at Reading since 2006, occupying a dual role as director of women's football and first-team manager until she left the club following its relegation in 2023. She had her second child that summer, and has become sporting director of the Utah Royals, who returned to the NSWL for the 2023–2024 season.

There have been plenty of times where we've sat and cried because we should have been at home with our kids. We talk a lot about having balance in our lives, and how easy it is to be too hard on ourselves.

It is great to have fellow leaders as allies. We appreciate the ferocity of the adrenaline hangovers, suffered in the Saturday-Tuesday-Saturday grind of the season. This might sound strange, but I was so proud of Kelly when her team beat mine 1–0 in December 2021. It was one of only two defeats we suffered in winning the WSL that season. I knew the restraints of her budget and had offered what advice I could in helping her to shape her recruitment strategy. She might describe me as a mentor, but we are really just very good friends.

You can imagine, then, my churning emotions on the final day of the 2022–2023 season, when my team beat hers to clinch the WSL title, and condemned Reading to relegation. I felt horribly conflicted as the final whistle blew. I immediately hugged my coaches and staff before doing the same with Kelly. It was a horrible conundrum, one that I would have given anything to avoid. Fate can be cruel, can't it?

Carla stepped down from her role in the summer of 2024 to prioritise her family life. She had been admirably open about the difficulty of balancing the demands of running an ambitious first-team program at a big club with being a fulfilling parent to her four-year-old daughter. She admits to struggling to stop work and was even negotiating with a potential signing at 5:00 p.m. on Christmas Eve. I understand those instincts, and if I can offer perspective through my own experiences, then great. It helps that I was taught to put myself in someone else's shoes from a young age.

I first reached out to Carla when she was at her previous club, Birmingham. She inherited a squad of only eight players and had to forfeit a match because they were unable to raise a team, but she did brilliantly to avoid relegation from the WSL before resigning on a point of principle.

That achievement drives home another of the realities of leadership. Pressure is a privilege, as Billie Jean King often pointed out, because it usually means there is an opportunity to excel. It also reveals cracks in your organization's culture and exposes weaknesses in mindset and preparation. It highlights the importance of having the right values, which cannot be abandoned under strain. It is the ultimate reality check. Resisting pressure doesn't guarantee you will have an easy time. It doesn't reduce the impact of adversity. It doesn't ensure that success is inevitable. When you feel the stress start to seize you, remember that everyone trips up and everyone falls down. Just don't stay on the floor for too long.

Develop an Interconnected Network

One of the many things I learned in America concerns net-working. It is a word I hear a lot, without it being fully understood. The true impact of networking is not how many people you have connected with but rather how many people you have connected to others in their orbit.

Sometimes it is good to say the unsayable and think the unthinkable with the people in your network. Another manager in the WSL called me to confide that they expected to lose their job. That took a lot of courage, and a humbling degree of trust in me. The conversation went something like this:

> **Me:** Why do you think you're going to get sacked?
> **Manager:** Well, you know how it is. We ain't won this. We ain't won that.
> **Me:** Why are you ringing me then?
> **Manager:** Well, what would you do if you were me?
> **Me:** Be proactive. I'd get on the phone to my chief exec. and ask to have lunch together ASAP. Tell him you'd love to have a catch-up, and that you're really looking forward to discussing plans for next season.

An hour later, the manager sent me a screenshot. The CEO had agreed to the meeting. The team won the following weekend. The pressure eased.

I've always tried to facilitate an environment of openness, challenge, and cohesion. Change at the right time is not necessarily a bad thing. There is a natural tendency to supress the difficult moments that occur in every team and workplace, as if they were unique to us.

They're not. Change happens everywhere. What are you going to do? Pretend everything is fine? It's not. It won't go away. Push down on the problem in an attempt to keep it out of sight and it will squeeze out sideways.

It is important to stress that when I talk to other managers I don't discuss game plans. I wouldn't say, "By the way, I'm thinking of exploiting your left back like this." In terms of teams and tactics, football is off the agenda. It has no part in the conversation. I discuss processes. How is the manager dealing with her challenges? What are her most important reference points? What is she about, as an individual? What is her team about, as a collective unit? The most important question is applicable to every workplace: who manages the manager?

It's not as simple as acquiring a mentor. It requires a mind shift. It is as if in modern business a leader is not allowed to have their own crisis. It's perfectly normal for a manager to worry if they are losing their grip or losing their way. It is not a sin to fret about being sacked or being found wanting. These are questions we are asking ourselves all the time, but we don't say them out loud.

Why not? What is so terrifying about an admission of vulnerability? Why should it be so difficult to accept? I'll tell you something for nothing: the unicorn theory of leadership does infinitely more harm than good.

Oh, and don't worry. If I'm not at my best I will have a word with myself, in the same way that I do with others.

In summary,

- nurture your friends.
- remember pressure is a privilege.
- develop an interconnected network.

Chapter 18

Embrace Failure, Extinguish Fear

Picture this scene. Imagine the look in the eyes of my Chelsea players when I ordered them to wear Arsenal shirts in training. They were puzzled, thrown off balance. Some were offended. Others seemed almost to pity me. It was as if I had finally tipped over the edge.

It had taken me a couple of years to get to that point—recognizing I had to do something stark to eradicate a fundamental inferiority complex. Arsenal had won their ninth consecutive league title during my first season in charge.

Although Arsenal had finished third the following year in 2013, they still lived rent free in my players' heads. We were a poor team, to be honest, and finished second from the bottom. I was in the process of dealing with weaknesses in talent and technique, but I knew I had to change the players' mindset.

There are very few new ideas in leadership, which, incidentally, is another reason to put the unicorn out of its misery. My brain wave was triggered by memories of an interview with Ian St. John and the enduring genius of Bill Shankly.

Shankly once insisted on switching Liverpool's kit to all red because, in the words of St. John, "he thought the colour scheme would carry psychological impact—red for danger, red for power." They wore it for the first time in a European Cup match against Anderlecht at Anfield on November 25, 1964.

St. John scored within ten minutes and Liverpool went on to win 3–0. Later that night, Shankly described the scene to his wife, Nessie. "There was a glow like a fire was burning," he told her. "Christ, the players looked like giants. And we played like giants."

He was convinced the psychological effect of color and noise was critical to the club's subsequent success. It helped that his initiative coincided with the development of color television, which highlighted the vividness of the all-red kit, and the forest of scarves, held aloft by supporters in the stands.

That theory is difficult to gauge, of course. Yet I was convinced it was not just another example of Shankly's flair for the showbiz sound bite. I had been Arsenal's women's assistant manager and Academy director for two years before going to the US, so I knew the attitude we were up against. Arsenal owned us.

In addition to distributing their shirts in training, I also pinned one up in the dressing room. I left pads of Post-it notes on the bench beneath the shirt and asked my players to write down what they thought it represented and stick their notes there.

It was then a case of waiting and watching to see if the seeds would germinate. Our seven-a-side practice matches were played between the reds and blues. When we went into 5-v-2 rondos, basically playing piggy in the middle, with the two in the middle wearing red and those on outside in blue.

My players might have kicked off when presented with my idea, but gradually the red shirt became just another shirt, instead of *that* shirt. It was fascinating to watch the mentality change via the messages they stuck onto the Arsenal top back in the dressing room. The feelings described by the early posters were predictable: *Nervous . . . angry . . . frustration.* But then attitudes began to harden: *Want to prove a point . . . overrated . . . old news . . . it's time for that team to step down.*

I had hung a Chelsea shirt on a nearby peg with the same invitation to stick Post-it notes on to it. It turned into a mind map: *Winners . . . ambitious . . . proud . . . respect . . . togetherness . . . creative . . . fresh . . . our time . . . blue sky . . . about to make winning permanent . . . a force . . . resilient . . . hard-working TEAM.*

Someone had put "team" in capitals for effect. We were on our way.

We wrenched the monkey off our backs by winning both league games against Arsenal in 2014 but lost to them 5–3 in the FA Cup semifinal. The pain of transition intensified when we blew the WSL title by losing at Manchester City on the final day.

The women's game was changing. We were in the process of going full time, and the bedrock of a successful culture was firm. Our winning streak began the following season in 2015, when we won the WSL and FA Cup double.

Don't Let Failure Get in Your Way

Moral of that particular story? The more times you do something the less you are afraid of it. People avoid fears because they are conditioned to avoid contamination by failure. To my mind that's completely self-defeating.

None of us is a paragon of perfection, even if your bum sinks into a nice leather boardroom chair at work and your executive washroom smells like a Parisian perfumery. I try hard to affect positivity to those around me but make more than my fair share of errors. Moaning about the mistakes I make is about as logical as complaining about the traffic noise when you buy a house next to a motorway. Listen to Michael Jordan, whose words should be imprinted on any leader's brain: "Limits, like fears, are often just an illusion."

It is essential to understand the psychological process of dealing with a direct threat or the onset of anxiety. Your limbic system, the primitive part of your brain wired for survival, kicks into gear. There are four main responses: flight, fight, freeze, or flock.

Flight is a considered choice. In other words, you weigh up the circumstances and run like hell. When you enter fight mode, you prepare to meet the challenge head on. Freezing involves playing dead so the aggressor leaves you alone. Think of the bird that goes limp in the mouth of a cat or the mouse that stiffens and becomes immobile when cornered. The body shuts down as a coping mechanism. You gamble that the best way to minimize harm is to wait for the threat to pass.

Flocking involves seeking out the comfort and safety of the collective. We see this work effectively in sports teams and support groups, in particular, where affinity is heightened by common experience. The sense of security encourages confidence, creativity, and informed decision-making.

There is a fifth response, fawning. This involves bending over backward to meet the demands of others, no matter how toxic they are as individuals and how damaging their demands may be. Such subservience sacrifices your needs and preferences in the vague hope of being excused. Try that in my world, and you will not last long.

Don't be afraid of the stumble or the setback. It is important to chart your failures, and absolutely critical that while you recognize that you learn the most from your mistakes you have mechanisms in place to ensure they do not happen again.

Let's take something as ultimately ephemeral as losing a game of football on a terrible pitch in torrid weather away from home against a team you should beat out of sight. You want excuses? You got 'em.

Conditions conspired against the better team. Normally crisp passes rolled imperfectly in the mire and rarely reached their target. The rain was biting into your bones. The wind did crazy things with ball flight. Self-talk becomes negative, so you are dragged down to your opponents' level.

Failure is a self-fulfilling prophesy. It starts when you are on the bus, traveling to the game. People look out of the rain-streaked windows and unconsciously start to exaggerate the conditions. They begin to mutter among themselves.

They don't fancy the challenge. They are afraid of seeming silly if they lose a match everyone expects them to win. They're looking for the get-out clause of a friendly pitch inspection. As a leader you have to read the danger signs, recognize the threat, and react accordingly.

I now refuse to discuss the possibility of postponement, even if, deep down, I know it is likely. My games are always on until they are off. If I get to a ground and the decision has yet to be made, I'll just roll a few balls out there to stress that the process of preparing to play is paramount. Stay on task, however attractive the temptation is to take the easy way out.

Emotional contagion works both ways. The odd raised eyebrow turns into a sigh and before you know it the group is consumed by a mushroom cloud of doubt, or worse, disinterest. People retreat into their hotel rooms or their work silos and zone out. Make sure that you are not responsible for spreading negative attitudes.

If the team leader or the CEO is having a bad day, the impact will be far greater on your people than you realize. When leaders walk around with a smile on their face, their evident sense of contentment and acknowledgment results in those around them smiling in return. Academic research bears out this natural tendency to copy others' actions and emotions. It has been recognized in babies within the first few months of life.

An experiment featuring Finnish students found that participants who were shown film clips of happy facial expressions had greater activity in their cheek muscles within 21 milliseconds. Those seeing angry or fearful facial expressions had increased muscular activity in their brows. Another experiment involved attaching sensors to the faces of volunteers, between their eyebrows, on their mouths, and on the corners of their jaws. This enabled psychologists to shape different emotional expressions. Those volunteers whose face was set in a frown reported feeling uneasy or unhappy.

Willem Verbeke, a Dutch academic, created four categories of people to explain how individuals react to stimulus. Charismatics reflect and radiate emotion, whereas empaths are emotionally engaged but less likely to infect others with their feelings. Expansives easily infect others but behave insensitively. Blands are unresponsive either way.

Friends or people who converse easily and are comfortable in each other's company speak at similar rates and similar lengths. They respond more readily to changes in posture or general body movements. In general, they are quicker to mirror each other.

This may not seem relevant to what you do in your everyday life, but it goes back to one of the eternal truths of leadership. Know your people.

There are layers of learning. When we reached the Champions League final in 2021, I felt so ready as a coach. But that ultimately didn't matter, because my Chelsea players were not as prepared as I felt. That was down to me because I hadn't delivered enough for them.

I thought I had perfected my game model. I had analyzed it so rigorously I could see pictures and patterns in my head. I had been ready to win the big prize for a long time, but it wasn't about my dreams and ambitions. I had failed to take my people with me. The match was over in twenty-one minutes: we were down 3–0 to Barcelona and conceded another goal before halftime. We had never played them before. It made us more vigilant, more aware, but perhaps not in the right way.

We were almost over-aroused. I saw the signs in the tunnel beforehand but could absolutely not believe the impact. It went against all the norms. There were no cozy theories to turn to, no simple solutions to pursue.

To be clear, if my teams lose, it will not be through lack of aggression. I want them to be naturally assertive. Yet on that night, I saw my most experienced players back off. It can only have been through fear and feeling intimidated.

We weren't ready to cope with what I have come to call big game challenges. It's essentially no different from making a presentation to the board or attending an important job interview. You are dry-mouthed, tightly wound, and nervous. The imagination runs riot.

My big insight following that wipe out in the biggest club match of all is not to cover up that nervousness. Let's not run away from it or camouflage its influence. Let's acknowledge it and prepare for it. Let's talk about our fears.

Process the Fear of Losing

Are you afraid of freezing in the biggest moment of your career? Are you worried you will be seized by stage fright? Are you privately obsessing about being unable to produce what's required of you? Are you petrified about being overcome by the occasion? Are you the introvert who says nothing in big meetings and in times of stress, and instead retreats deeper into yourself? Don't worry. It's natural, not a mortal sin. There are many emotional obstacles to overcome.

In the days before a massive occasion, you will be thinking about it all the time. You will probably dream about it. Your brain overheats. You will convince yourself you are going to be unable to kick the ball. You cannot envisage scoring the type of goal you usually pull off without thinking. In your workplace, you might be rehearsing your presentation for your next sales conference, convinced you'll forget your glasses or scared your voice will shake. The greater the exposure, the more fearful you may become.

Let's front-end that problem. Accept that addressing your heads of department once a year is not just another meeting, just like playing in the Champions League final is not just another game. Neither is playing in a World Cup, Olympic, or European Championship final, for that matter. Playing at Wembley, a traditional fantasy for any football-mad kid, is a big deal.

The knots in the stomach will still be there, despite the familiarity of the surroundings. The butterflies will be fluttering, no matter how many times you file out of the dressing room and hear the hum of a large, expectant crowd.

Yet, as your coach, I'll be in your ear, telling you the more you experience these types of games, the easier it becomes. My job is not only to make sure I am ready for the occasion, but also to ensure you are equipped with the tools to be able to deal with it.

Before crucial moments in your career, turn to your truth tellers, the mentors, and the trusted friends for their honest input and their emotional support. Every time you push yourself, you get better. Remember, paralysis and passivity is not going to propel you forward. Proactivity is what you need.

That's not a quick fix or an overnight sensation. You can recruit a team, develop its characteristics, and push individuals so relentlessly that the team reaches a Cup final, but you have to deal with the importance of the big occasion in an overt way. The key to success in that key moment is emotional rather than tactical or technical. That means you have to process the fear of losing.

You must condition your players to walk out in front of ninety thousand people. They might not have eaten well in the build-up to the match. They almost certainly will have had disturbed sleep patterns. It's traumatic, and a moment of truth. Who are you when life is that much harder?

I won't minimize the downsides.

Antoine Griezmann admits he still wakes up at random moments in the middle of the night and can recall in minute detail the horror of hitting the crossbar with a penalty shot for Atlético de Madrid against Real Madrid in the 2016 Champions League final, which they lost in a shoot-out.

Sport often offers second chances, but you do not always get the opportunity to atone for your error or underperformance. I still look back at our Champions League final in 2021 as a huge missed opportunity, but because leaders must also look at themselves in the first instance, I realize I didn't fully appreciate what my players were dealing with.

Do I think they were the better for the experience? Undoubtedly. Do I think that if they were playing in the Champions League or World Cup final tomorrow every one of my players would be prepared for the extreme level of scrutiny and the implications of playing well or poorly?

Not all of them, to be honest, but each will be better equipped, in any way, shape, or form. The flame of failure has passed through, around, and between them. That collective experience is searing, but significant.

Make Preparation Your Daily Ritual

It is no coincidence that Barcelona had suffered a heavy defeat to Lyon in their previous Champions League final in 2019. They had an almost feral look about them when they faced us on that humbling night in Gothenburg two years later. Scarred by the pain of previous disappointment, they played with revealing ferocity and a cold ruthlessness.

The team I fear the most is the one that knows what it is to lose when it hurts the most. Those players will have worked on their own coping strategies. Their coaches will have been consumed by the challenge of picking up the pieces and making them whole. Enforced renewal is, by its nature, uniquely powerful.

The best leadership group involves everyone, but so much is down to the individual. One of my players who had a particularly difficult time against Barcelona didn't sleep for two nights after the game. She basically hid under her pillow. She had to wait nearly two years before facing the opponent who had caused her such mental pain in that final once again. I simply told her the crushingly obvious: this was her chance to kill the demon. Oh my, did she take it.

She was superb. Her tormentor didn't get a kick. When she came off the pitch no words were needed between us. I know the private work that underpins such public healing. Preparation had been a daily ritual, because the memory of her failure had never let her rest. She was driven by the moment and came back from the lowest point in her career.

Redemption is beautiful to behold. It is a process that takes time, examines character, and rewards personal growth. We were beaten again by Barcelona in the 2023 Champions League semifinal by 2–1 on aggregate after losing the first leg at home by a single goal, but it was a source of pride and reassurance, a reminder of how far we had come and how far we had to go.

We were the better team in the 1–1 draw at Camp Nou in Barcelona, where they had been unbeaten for four years. I could hear their coaches panicking on the touchline. Their manager was even cautioned by the referee for his histrionics. The experience told me the gap was closing.

It takes a lot for people to admit that they might be afraid or to acknowledge the suspicion they're not good enough. A leader's task is to provide reassurance, deliver sweet reasoning, and enable them to recognize the prize that is in the palm of their hands. Just as people learn in different ways, they deal with their insecurities in contrasting fashion. Some will still look at an opponent and agonize, deep down, that they are inferior. This is just an emotional reaction. It is manageable because it can be controlled through an acknowledgment of that fear.

I've been through my own trials and tribulations. I worked through my fears before undergoing an emergency hysterectomy. It was easier for me to face because I'd already had surgery for my C-section, so I had a clear idea of what was ahead. I learned how to recover. I was aware I could do absolutely nothing in the first two weeks following surgery. I couldn't rush through the first six weeks of rehabilitation. I didn't dash back to work because of the potential long-term impact to my health.

The 2022–2023 season was the hardest in my experience, but one of the most rewarding. To do the League and FA Cup double again was a testament to the collective character of a group that responds well to adversity and challenge. We took a potential negative, a congested schedule, and turned it into a positive because we thrived on the pressure that created.

I'm not immune to the strain of the job. I understand why elite coaches do a few years in a particular role and then get off the train for a bit. They've probably got $10 million in the bank. I haven't.

Eventually I will do something else with my life. I am already committed to stretching myself, on different terms, with the US national team. I have always been interested in leadership and performance, particularly involving female athletes. I like being around adults with similar mindsets. Perhaps in the years to come that will guide me toward a wider executive role in a new era for the women's game.

I feel I am drawing the strands of my life together. There is no bigger cause than responding to climate change. Seas are rising at an unimaginable rate, and parts of our world are going to be underwater in twenty-five years. I find a series of existential questions compelling.

How are we going to change human behavior, since without that change we are headed toward catastrophe? How are we going to persuade governments, multinational corporations, and entire industries to look beyond dangerously narrow self-interest?

How are we going to decrease human consumption of energy? How are we going to rid ourselves of our reliance on oil? How can we develop a consensus behind an alternative strategy? I look at Harry and worry that we are already too late.

I can't believe how quickly time passes. There's always more to come, even if I don't know what form that will take. I'm not that old, and I'm certainly not ready to be put out to pasture. I have been blessed.

I have no regrets, personally or professionally. I know I've been telling you there's no such thing as perfection, but achieving peace of mind comes very close. Reports of my invincibility have been hopelessly exaggerated.

Epilogue

Future Proof

I know it is a corny old line, but Old Trafford really was the Theatre of Dreams on that rare sunny Saturday in May 2024. I had the luxury of contemplating greatness from the touchline during the game as I looked over the pitch and up, across the stand named in honour of Sir Alex Ferguson, the coach I most admire.

The win over Manchester United, and our fifth successive WSL title, was secure. Two goals up in eight minutes, four goals ahead at halftime, our lead stretched to five two minutes into the second half. I was lost in the moment long before Fran Kirby, Chelsea's record goal scorer, added a sixth in her final appearance for the club.

I was in Sir Alex's home. I felt his presence in the posh seats behind me when I looked back to share the occasion with the travelling fans who had our back in tough times. I thought of the standards he instilled, the values he represented, the wisdom he espoused over twenty-seven years.

His longevity befits his legend. It is a source of enduring regret that, because of the post-match melee, we never got to share the glass of red wine we had promised ourselves. I'm conscious that, as a fellow coach, I'm privileged to have the opportunity to stand on the shoulders of such a giant.

Given the context of my final season at Chelsea, that WSL title, our eighth in ten years when you take the Covid-era Spring Series into account, stands as my greatest managerial achievement. Watching my team demonstrate everything our programme represented, decisively and under the most intense pressure, was impossibly poignant.

The group endured a series of gut punches. The loss of Sam Kerr to injury, and having Millie Bright out for so long, stripped a transitional team of experience. The disappointment of defeat to Arsenal in the League Cup final, to a single goal late in extra time, was compounded by semi-final losses to Manchester United in the FA Cup and Barcelona in the Champions League.

They are a special set of human beings. I had to teach them important lessons in adversity, remind them that success doesn't come without a struggle. The collective character they showed proved they had listened to my mantra that reputation and past achievement offer no guarantee of a medal around your neck.

There's a lot of loose talk about legacy, but I'm proud of winning while developing young players of the quality of Maika Hamano and Aggie Beever-Jones and easing seasoned players into more unaccustomed supporting roles for the common good.

Forget the obsession with style, a coach's ego trip. This group proved you can't win football matches playing the same way every time. They did what they needed to do, despite the daunting logic that odds were against them.

There have been nonsensical suggestions I was indulging in mind games when I effectively conceded the title after we lost at Liverpool on May 1, seventeen days before the season's climax. I was merely dealing in realities, because had we enjoyed the advantage given to Manchester City by that loss, we would have got the job done.

Instead, the following Sunday, I sat in the car outside our Kingsmeadow ground with Denise Reddy listening to City's late defeat to Arsenal. "We're going to do this," I told her as we made our way into the dressing room before our late home game against Bristol City.

The atmosphere was electric. The door was ajar and metaphorically kicked in by an 8-0 win that gave us a favourable goal difference, that was extended in the two remaining games. We squeezed the last drop out of the lemon.

I certainly had nothing left to give. The marrow had been sucked dry. I had spoken several times to Jürgen Klopp, who was enduring his own farewell tour at Liverpool, about the mind-numbing tiredness our job generates.

We related to each other on a visceral level and vowed that things in our profession had to change. It has reached the point where the expectations and obligations are actively detrimental to a coach's mental health.

Leadership involves the management of emotion. I was obviously conscious that it was my last season at Chelsea, but I couldn't allow that to set the tone. I condensed my approach, so that I concentrated only on what was important. I found that quite liberating.

My focus was on the people I worked with, the players and the fans. I spent more time with supporters, before and after matches. I redoubled my efforts in creating the best possible environment for my squad, knowing that our time together was finite and precious.

I stayed away from the politics of everything else. I took extraneous matters, commercial considerations, marketing campaigns, the wider issues of the game's development, out of the equation. I returned to a place that had been increasingly hard for me to reach as the Chelsea project evolved.

I rediscovered the value of a purity of purpose.

My successors will not have to deal with the bullshit I had to deal with in my twelve years in charge at Chelsea. They will not have to fight to play on a properly tended pitch, prepare in decent dressing rooms, and work out in an appropriately equipped gym.

They won't have to move stadiums, fight to be established under the main banner of the football club, rather than being regarded as an offshoot of its charitable foundation. Soon after I departed, Chelsea announced a new long-term strategy for the women's team, designed to facilitate an eight-figure budget. Mine improved incrementally from £65,000 to £150,000, £250,000 to £400,000, £1.2m to £2m, £4m to £5m.

In my early days, I helped to roll pitches at Staines to get a game on. I paid for meals, even paid for players. I paid Sofia Jakobsson's £5,000 transfer fee out of my own money in 2013, through a foreign exchange business I ran. I never got it back, by the way...

I really wanted to build something. I know leaders say they want to leave things in a better place for those who follow them through the door. That's a given. But I wanted to leave Chelsea in a place where all my successor had to do was focus on being a football coach and manager.

I had a choice to make in creating a culture. Do the other stuff, the irritating and distracting stuff, or let everyone suffer because there was no one else to do it. I always had Paul Green, my general manager, by my side, but I had to lead from the front.

We built a club from the ground up. We went from being just about in the top one hundred in the world to definitely being in the top three in the world. We made a Champions League final with a budget of £2 million. Barcelona, our opponents, worked with £15m. Lyon, perennial winners, was given £20m a season.

This book hopefully highlights my belief in humanity. I did get teary, driving into training in those final months, thinking about someone else leading my group. I had to work so hard at not feeling anxious about what I was losing. I pushed myself to feel excited for those players. They have a new chapter to write, a new voice to respond to, much in the same way I will be thrilled by my new environment.

I also know those bonds are never going to be broken. We talk about teams as families, and sometimes that can be translated literally. To give an example, I looked at Facebook recently, and saw one of my former players, Emily Martin, who retired to the US, had just had her second child. I started crying, recalling how she went through a stage in her life and career when she looked a little lost. I worried so much about her, but to see her looking so happy made me realize I will remain in the lives of the players I left behind at Chelsea. I will watch out for them.

I will watch the team from afar, as a fan. I just hope they invite me to their cup finals, as a guest. I'd love to be on the halfway line, close to them when they lift their trophies. I look forward to watching the progress of a new generation.

The club will remain part of my family's life. My niece Isabella wouldn't speak to me for a couple of weeks after I got the US job. Those Chelsea players were her role models.

I see great NFL coaches, like Bill Belichick and Pete Carroll, creating and leaving dynasties. I asked myself whether I wanted to stay on as long as Sir Alex at Manchester United. I genuinely thought I'd be at Chelsea for life, progressing from coaching to being sporting director and board member, but it hasn't worked out that way. Sixteen trophies in twelve years will have to do.

You probably won't be surprised to learn there is another photograph on my kitchen wall that means an awful lot to me. It is of our first FA Cup final win in 2015 against Notts County. The final whistle has just blown. Rick Passmoor, an old school manager but a consistent ally and a great guy, turns in disappointment to his staff on the County bench. To his right, Ji So-Yun, who had scored the game's only goal, leaps high in the air. A two-man TV crew, a sign of burgeoning interest, homes in on her exultation. A couple of feet away Katie Chapman, a leader and mother, dives on to my back, giving me whiplash. On the lefthand edge of the frame, the fourth official starts to stride towards the pitch. I knew on that day Rebecca Welch would be a star. With significantly less experience than me, in my field, she went on to become the first female referee of a Premier League game, just before Christmas 2023.

That's progress. I'm not taking anything away from her, but we should not shy away from asking why such welcome development is possible in officiating but not, it seems, in coaching. How, and more pertinently why, is that possible?

It's a scratched record conversation. It doesn't move. We might pick up the needle now and again, but it goes to the same place. It catches a little bit of fluff. We might hit the next track occasionally, but it always reverts to the beginning.

We have to ask ourselves fundamental questions. Why is that? It has nothing to do with talent.

So much misogyny is stage managed through social media. It's painful and tiring to be subjected to it. Over the last year, I have never felt more exhausted by the amount of casual sexism I have experienced. The higher I have climbed the ladder, the worse it has got. The level of scrutiny to which you are exposed means you have to ask yourself whether it is worth it.

It is almost as if I am regarded as an existential threat, instead of a colleague with great experience. It confronts you in so many ways. On one level I try to understand it, in that some people are threatened by points of difference, but it all comes back to education and self-awareness.

So many people are so unaware of their ignorance, of how little they know, and how susceptible they are to bias. The familiarity of maleness feels natural to them. But the broader lesson is that we must all evolve or die.

People parrot complaints about cancel culture or a supposed lack of freedom of speech. That's so much nonsense. You can more or less say what you like on social media. Accountability is a convenient myth for grifters, malcontents, and cowards. No one is going to take their platform away. They're unaware that for so long all the food has been on one huge table, set for the same people. The rest of us are clustered around small tables, hoping for scraps and crumbs. We should intermingle more. It's healthy. A more diverse ecosystem offers greater choice and opportunity.

I believe in dynamic environments. I can't wrap my head around the fact elite sport is so one-dimensional. It lacks balance in so many different ways. A healthy society and a healthy atmosphere are the result of difference, whether that is male or female, Black or white.

Everybody in the room is the same. Footballers deal with emotional problems, suppressed insecurity. Countering that is not necessarily about a woman's touch. I could go into a dressing room and deal with sensitive issues in the same way that Ian Wright, my friend and soul mate, could do so.

Oh, by the way, women can work in a men's dressing room without wanting to sleep with them.

I cannot imagine myself coaching in the WSL again, although when I do come back from the States I will do so as a supporter of my club, watching every week. Who knows, I may be so enriched by my experiences in international football that I enter the men's game. I can't rule that out, regardless of the damage caused by so much crude misogyny.

That isn't necessarily about what I want but rather about clubs and owners being prepared to take the leap of faith. I don't want to get too far ahead of myself, but after a minimum of five years with the USWNT, I will have a skill set beyond many of my male counterparts.

I understand the realities. It is easier for Nick Cushing to go from Manchester City, in the women's game, to Red Bull Leipzig, or for Tony Gustavsson, the Matilda's coach, to become assistant manager of the Swedish men's team. They're male. I'm disadvantaged just because I am female.

When you have grown up, and all you have known, seen, and heard are people who look and sound like you, attitudes are shaped accordingly. Change can be threatening.

We talk a lot about representation in sport, and the realities are that football, in terms of senior management and leadership, has never been representative of our society. We have seen the struggle year on year of Black and ethnic minority coaches and candidates to make a breakthrough.

I remember a therapist once telling me that the more you push something down, the more it squeezes out sideways. That's how I feel when I consider how many more blocks or excuses or diversions are going to be created before someone sees the value in change. Our game needs to be future-proofed by the provision of opportunity for all.

I can't see it happening in England—where the merry-go-round of mediocrity still spins—for a long time. But I can see it happening in the US, for sure. I'm emboldened and energised by the challenge I've taken on. Let's hope, to borrow another line from my first presentation to my US players and staff, the tables are starting to turn.

Acknowledgments

This book may capture my personality and philosophy, but it is given its depth by my family, friends, and a variety of fantastic people who have helped me on my way. I'm not going to let this opportunity to thank them slip by.

My son, Harry, gave me a bigger meaning and purpose in life, and our unconditional love means more than I can say. If I can be half as good a parent to him as my mum and dad were to me, I will be blessed. His aunts, my sisters Becky and Victoria, are in that circle of love.

Perspective comes from my best friend, Kirsty Pealling, and other close pals, like Jenny Canty, Becky Antoniou, and Rhian Monteith, whom I have known since uni. Professionally, I will always be in debt to Vic Akers, Mr. Arsenal. Thanks also to Laura Ferri, Nicole Taney, David Hershey, and Amanda Vandervort.

Players, past and present, have given me their all. I cannot ask for more. My staff have worked wonders in various settings over the years, and I particularly value the closeness of the professional relationships I established at Chelsea with Paul Green, Denise Reddy, Stuart Searle, and Bart Caubergh. Bruce Buck's wisdom and guidance were invaluable, and the diligence of Nicky Anderson made a hectic schedule manageable.

I like to think Mike, my cowriter, and I make a good team, but we have the teams behind this book to thank. Jo Tongue and all at Tongue Tied Management make my life so much easier. Rory Scarfe, at the Blair Partnership in London, and Sarah Passick, at Park & Fine in New York, played key roles in bringing our work to market. Christine Preston transcribed countless hours of conversation to make this happen.

Thanks, finally, to the team at PublicAffairs, led by Clive Priddle and including, at various junctures, Kimberly Meilun, Lindsay Fradkoff, Jaime Leifer, and Brooke Parsons. Their expertise and insight have been invaluable. I hope you enjoy the fruits of their collective labor.

—Emma Hayes

Index

Emma Hayes was appointed head coach of the US Women's National Team in November 2023, signing a five-year contract. She fulfilled her responsibilities as Chelsea manager before taking charge in the final phase of preparations for the 2024 Olympic Games.

Her iconic management career began with the Long Island Lady Riders in the United States where, as the youngest female head coach in W-League history, she was named National Coach of the Year in 2002.

Emma was honored as Metro Atlantic Athletic Conference Coach of the Year in 2004 before she returned to England, where, as assistant first team coach and academy director, she helped Arsenal Women win eleven major trophies over three seasons.

A second spell in the US saw her serve as head coach and director of football operations at Chicago Red Stars, coaching consultant at Washington Freedom, and technical director at New York Flash before she was named manager of Chelsea in June 2012.

Her teams defined an era of unparalleled expansion in women's football in the UK. Under her leadership, Chelsea won the Women's Super League seven times (2015, 2018, 2020, 2021, 2022, 2023, and 2024)and the women's FA Cup five times (2015, 2018, 2021, 2022, and 2023).

She was named World Coach of the Year by FIFA, and her passionate advocacy led to her being given the MBE for her services to football in the Queen's 90th Birthday Honours in 2016. She received an OBE in the Queen's New Year Honours List in 2022 in recognition of her continued influence on the women's game.

An award-winning television pundit, intuitive leader, and prominent campaigner on women's welfare issues, this is her first book.

Michael Calvin, her collaborator, is an award-winning writer and internationally best-selling author. His books, which feature several sports and include a globally acclaimed Holocaust memoir, have been hailed for their insight and influence.